# My Friend Miss

## A Comedy

Donald Churchill
and
Peter Yeldham

*Samuel French – London*
*New York – Sydney – Toronto – Hollywood*

ISBN 978-0-573-11271-3

www.samuelfrench-london.co.uk

www.samuelfrench.com

---

### FOR AMATEUR PRODUCTION ENQUIRIES

### UNITED KINGDOM AND WORLD
### EXCLUDING NORTH AMERICA
plays@SamuelFrench-London.co.uk
020 7255 4302/01

Each title is subject to availability from Samuel French,

depending upon country of performance.

---

# MY FRIEND MISS FLINT

First presented at the Theatre Royal, Windsor on 1st March, 1983 with the following cast of characters:

| | |
|---|---|
| **Tom Lambert** | Tony Anholt |
| **Lucy** | Linda Regan |
| **Albert** | Jack Smethurst |
| **Sarah** | Virginia Stride |
| **Mr Dodds** | Dennis Ramsden |
| **C. P. Lens** | Mona Bruce |

The play directed by Hugh Goldie
Designed by John Page


The setting is a studio/apartment in a converted riverside warehouse.

ACT I
   Scene 1   Morning
   Scene 2   Early afternoon

ACT II
   Scene 1   Mid-afternoon
   Scene 2   Late afternoon

Time — the present

# ACT I

## Scene 1

*A studio/apartment on an upper floor of a converted riverside warehouse in East London. Morning*

*There is a window set in the upstage wall, through which we see the north side of the river . . . office blocks . . . perhaps a distant glimpse of the Post Office Tower. Next to the window is the front door, which is glazed in panels of clear glass. The main living area comprises a modern Habitat-type sofa and a fifteen-year-old Charles Eames leather chair. It is a mixture of the good and the shabby giving a general impression that the flat is occupied by an untidy but prosperous bachelor. Attached to one part of the upstage wall is a sort of conservatory with an open end facing us. At this end is a workbench bearing assorted plants and horticultural equipment. Next to this is a plastic noteboard.* DR *is the door to the bathroom and near it, an archway leading to the bedroom.* L *is a door to the kitchen*

*The decor is mainly bare brick. On the walls are assorted framed photographs of Tom in various gardens. In some of them he is with Percy Thrower and other gardening gurus of the media. Among the pictures and paintings is a gouache and coloured pencil drawing of three women on a beach. It is by Picasso and it is the identity of the artist rather than his subject which is most apparent*

*When the* CURTAIN *rises, the apartment curtains are half-drawn but in the gloom we can make out the shapes of furniture. The silence is broken by the sound of, an ice-cream van playing "Greensleeves" very quickly and then breaking off abruptly. Silence. The song starts again*

**Tom** (*off*) Shut up!

*The music stops. A pause of four seconds then it resumes*

(*Off*) Right! That's it!

*Tom enters from the bedroom pulling on tracksuit trousers and top*

That's the second time this week he's woken me up.

*The music stops. Tom stops. Then the Ice-cream Man sings an unaccompanied solo*

**Man** (*off; singing*) "Just one Cornetto!"

*"Greensleeves" music resumes. Tom slips on empty bottles as he makes his way to the door. He flings it open and steps out on the catwalk and shouts down*

**Tom** I'll give you one more Cornetto mate! If I have to come down there, I'll give you a knuckle sandwich!

*The music stops instantly. Tom comes back in. Then a few defiant bars of "Colonel Bogey" from the van. Tom runs out. The van is heard starting up and driving off. Tom returns and draws back the curtains. He surveys the room. It is the morning after a party with empty bottles, used plates, etc. Half-heartedly he starts to pick up some of the debris*

> *As he does so, Lucy Napier enters from the bedroom tying the cord of a man's shortie travelling-robe. Lucy is a bright, perky-looking girl of about thirty. A Londoner*

**Lucy** 'Ello!

**Tom** Good-morning! (*He covers his upper nakedness by pulling up his tracksuit trousers to his chest*) It's probably a little late in the day to introduce myself but——

**Lucy** You're Tom Lambert.

**Tom** Ah! Yes ... well ... it *is* too late!

**Lucy** Bet you don't know who I am though.

**Tom** Certainly! I know who you *are* ... you rang my bell last night. I remember that because I remember thinking you were the nicest person I've had on my door-step for months.

**Lucy** What's my name?

**Tom** Ah! Now you were from er ...

**Lucy** McDonalds.

**Tom** The hamburger people?

**Lucy** McDonald's Market Research. I'm doing a survey on "Alcohol and Creativity".

**Tom** It's all coming back.

**Lucy** You said "We're having a party. Come in and have a gin and tonic and maybe we'll get creative later."

**Tom** So I was quite nice to you?

**Lucy** Very. We had a few drinks, then we all went out for a nosh and ended up at the *Laughing Bear*. How do you feel this morning?

**Tom** Like a bear with a sore head.

**Lucy** Then we came back here and played forfeits. I lost.

**Tom** You didn't lose anything else? I mean, I hope I didn't take advantage of you because if I did, I don't remember a thing about it. That's what would upset me ... doing it and not remembering.

**Lucy** You said I was the best thing that'd happened to you in years?

**Tom** Did I?

**Lucy** That I was sensational ...

**Tom** Right ...

**Lucy** The sort of girl you'd been looking for all your life?

**Tom** Yes ... that's right. Sensational. You can't seriously think I'd forget a single thing about you, my darling.

**Lucy** What's my name?

**Tom** Er ... (*He pauses*) ... ah now, come on ... don't be like that.

*She waits. He smiles and opens his mouth as if to make an announcement. Then stares at her, baffled.*

It begins with an L. Definitely with an L. Llll ... no, don't help me ... Llll ...

*She glares unhelpfully*

It's there on the tip of my tongue ... Llll ... it's coming ... Lllaaa ... Lllee ... Lii ... Lllo ... Lilo? No, that can't be right. Give me a clue. Just a small one.

**Lucy** Llluuu ...

**Tom** Of course! Got it! Say no more. (*He sings à la Maurice Chevalier*) "Every leetle breeze seems to whisper Louise——"

**Lucy** LUCY!

**Tom** "—whisper Luceee" ... (*He gives a Gallic shrug*) I remember it well.

*The telephone rings. Both ignore it as he smiles at her. Lucy pouts a kiss at him, as if she forgives him, then backs from him, pulling out the elasticized top of his track-suit trousers an alarming distance*

Here ... don't do that ... steady on ...

*Lucy lets go. It winds him. She exits to the bathroom, slamming the door behind her*

*Tom, tenderly rubbing his stomach, picks up the phone*

(*On the phone*) Hello? ... Speaking. ... Yes, Thomas Lambert. Who's that? ... Good-morning, Mr Dodds, what can I do for you? ... Inland Revenue? ... Oh, you want my accountant. Her number is— ... Who? ... Miss Flint? No, I—oh just a minute. (*Covering the receiver he calls towards the bathroom*) Louise!

*The door opens and Lucy comes out with a toothbrush in hand, halfway through cleaning her teeth*

**Lucy** Lucy.

**Tom** Exactly! That's right. And your surname ... don't tell me ... let me guess ... it's all coming back ... is ... (*triumphantly*) Flint!

**Lucy** Who?

**Tom** Flint.

**Lucy** Very nearly. My name is Napier. Lucy Napier.

**Tom** That's what I thought. And that toothbrush is the one I use for cleaning my tennis shoes.

*Lucy exits to the bathroom, slamming the door behind her*

*Tom flinches, then uncovers the receiver and speaks into the phone*

(*On the phone*) I'm sorry Mr Napier— ... Mr Dodds, I do beg your pardon—no, there is no Miss Flint here. ... Miss Joanna Flint? (*Cheerfully*) I can honestly say I've never heard of her. You must have the wrong number. ... Not at all. Goodbye. (*He hangs up and calls towards the bathroom door*) I think I'll go for a jog.

**Lucy** (*off*) For a what?

**Tom** My morning jog. To clear my head. Help yourself to anything you need. (*He moves rather wearily towards the front door*)

*Lucy enters*

**Lucy** I'll tidy up. Where do you keep your Hoover?

**Tom** Oh, don't bother about that. My cleaner comes in today. I shan't be long.

*Tom exits*

*Lucy starts to gather up her scattered clothing. She notices the Picasso above the sideboard and peers at the signature. She stands back and appraises it. Impressed, she continues to pick up her clothes, finishing near Tom's desk. A silver bowl on an adjacent bookcase catches her attention; she turns it over and squints at the bottom. Picking up a magnifying glass from the desk, she examines the hallmark on the bowl*

**Lucy** EPNS.

*She replaces the bowl and locates the rest of her clothing. Obviously something is missing. She looks around, puzzled, then spots her knickers high up on a climbing plant. She tries to reach. Then gets a chair. She places it by the trellis and stands on it. She still cannot reach. She tests the trellis with her foot. It holds her but as she goes to climb up, the chair revolves. She clutches the trellis as the chair falls over. She considers her position for a moment. The trellis gives a slight creak but seems secure. She stretches up gingerly but the pants are still out of reach. She carefully climbs up another two rungs*

  *Albert appears on the catwalk and searches for his key. He opens the door and enters. Albert is middle-aged; wears an old mac and cap and is carrying a grip. A non-descript man, world-weary, and on the seedy side*

*Neither Lucy or Albert see each other. Albert surveys the debris as he slowly removes his mac and cap and hangs them up in the cupboard. Underneath he wears an old cardigan with suede patches which, judging by the crude stitches, he has sewn on himself. His trousers are ancient cavalry twill. Around the neck of his frayed Viyella shirt is some kind of club tie ... all of which give him the air of a cashiered major. There is a sharp crack of splintering wood from the trellis. He turns and sees Lucy spreadeagled five feet up on the trellis and hanging on fearfully. He goes to speak, but stops. He goes closer to her and admires her rear view. There is another sharp crack of snapping wood*

  Oh 'eck! (*She lowers her leg to a lower rung. Another crack. She gives a little scream*) Help! I'm falling.

*Another crack ... louder than the others. Albert lunges his hands against her thighs. She screams much louder at this*

**Albert** That's all right, miss. I gotcha! You're in safe hands. I'm Mr Lambert's daily. Put your other leg just here, miss. (*He holds her legs and guides her down*) That's right. You're doing well. That's right ... just there ... and the other one here. Put yourself in my hands.

*She reaches the ground. He still holds her legs*

**Lucy** Thank you.

*He does not move*

I'm down now.
**Albert** Yes.
**Lucy** Thanks very much.
**Albert** My pleasure, miss. Don't mention it. (*He steps away*)
**Lucy** I was trying to get my things up there.
**Albert** No problem, miss. Mr Lambert did a programme the other month on pruning apple trees. We've got just the thing.

*Albert goes to the conservatory section and comes out with a long pruning pole. He brings the knickers down on the end of it and lowers the pole to her. She takes them*

**Lucy** Ta.

*He replaces the pole*

You Mr Lambert's daily?
**Albert** Well, to be precise, his twice-weekly.
**Lucy** A sort of char lady?
**Albert** A char person. We're all persons now, miss.
**Lucy** Of course. Sorry.
**Albert** It's not my regular line of work, of course. (*He picks up the waste-paper bin and begins collecting bottles, emptying ashtrays, etc.*) That has been effectively torpedoed by young, up-start TV producers who wouldn't know a true professional from a hole in their lens aperture.
**Lucy** Oh, you're an actor?
**Albert** Very nearly. Oh yes, for many years I enjoyed a most interesting living in the performing arts. I started with a bang. Got rave reviews when I was at Butlins. Filey nineteen fifty-eight.
**Lucy** What else have you done?
**Albert** Well, I was in *Aladdin on Ice* at Wembley. Widow Twankey's understudy. But I had a bit of bad luck there. The one time I had to go on, it was my birthday and I was celebrating with a few quiet brandies in my dressing-room when the stage manager rushed in and told me to put my skates on. It was a Thursday matinee. The Mayor and Mayoress of Wembley were paying us a special visit. I took one step on the ice, went arse over tip and ended up in the Mayoress's lap with both my tits burst. Yes, I've had my share of bad luck in life. I've always been good, mind you . . . good but unlucky. And luck is more important than talent in my game. (*He produces a pair of tights from behind the sofa*) You're probably looking for these, miss.
**Lucy** Ta. Don't you have an agent to get you work?
**Albert** My agent? Please . . . don't speak ill of the dead.
**Lucy** I'm sorry. Did he die recently?
**Albert** He might just as well have done for all the good he does me. When I

phoned him three years ago, his secretary said he was out to lunch but would ring me back. I waited three years, then, when I phoned him last Tuesday, he was still out to lunch. I said to his secretary he must have finished his cheese and biscuits by now. I got a letter next day saying they no longer wished to represent me because I was a trouble-maker.

**Lucy** What a shame. The arts ain't easy, are they? I'm an artist myself, so I do know. I won this scholarship to art school but I couldn't get it together.

**Albert** You've got to be versatile these days if you want to earn your living by expressing yourself.

**Lucy** Like you doing this cleaning job?

**Albert** Oh I couldn't manage on what 'is nibs pay me. He makes Scrooge look like the last of the big spenders. I'll let in some fresh air.

*Albert opens the door*

**Lucy** Tom was very generous to me last night.

**Albert** He would be. He's very nice to nice people.

**Lucy** Aren't you nice? I think you're nicer than you look.

**Albert** Me? Don't you kid yourself, miss. He knows I'll do him if I get half a chance.

**Lucy** Why don't he sack you?

**Albert** He thinks he'll convert me in time. Like all do-gooders . . . he's sure he knows best.

**Lucy** How long you been coming here?

**Albert** Three years. He's always nagging me about my evil ways. But it suits me coming here 'cos it's near the *Queen Adelaide* . . . the pub on the corner.

**Lucy** You like to drink there?

**Albert** No, I entertain there every Friday and Saturday.

**Lucy** Fabulous!

**Albert** You wouldn't say that if you saw my act, but it pays the rent.

**Lucy** What do you do?

**Albert** Nothing special. Sing a few songs, mime to a record, tell a few jokes, and end up doing a comedy strip-tease. Come and see me. Fridays and Saturdays. Albert Larkin I'm known as professionally. Albert Larkin, the merchant of mirth . . . certified insanely funny.

**Lucy** Sounds terrific. Well, I think I'll have a shower, and get dressed.

**Albert** Certainly, miss. It's right in there. I'll get you a towel. (*He fetches one from the cupboard*) Here you are.

**Lucy** Ta.

*Lucy takes the towel and exits into the bathroom*

*Albert brings out a vacuum cleaner and begins to hoover. After a few moments there is a scream from the bathroom*

**Albert** Oh my God!

*He rushes into the bathroom*

(*Off*) I should have warned you, miss.

*There is another scream and Albert backs out, wiping water off himself*

Yes, I'm sorry about that, miss. That's a very funny shower. There are two wheels to activate——

*The door slams in his face*

—the water pressure and that big lever adjusts the temperature.

*A slight pause*

> *Lucy puts her head round the door*

**Lucy** Ta. It's working great now.

> *The door shuts as Lucy goes back into the bathroom*

**Albert** Oh good! Excellent! Yes ... sorry about that, miss. It's a very old shower you see.

*Albert returns to his hoovering but stops and eyes the bathroom door. He hoovers over there. He bends and looks through the keyhole, then takes the nozzle off the vacuum cleaner and holds it to the keyhole*

> *During this, Sarah appears at the open door*

*Albert checks the keyhole, then vacuums it again. Sarah sees this as she enters. She is an attractive if slightly brisk woman in her late thirties. She carries a briefcase and handbag. Albert is totally unaware of her as he settles to look through the keyhole. He turns off the vacuum and looks through the keyhole again*

**Sarah** Good-morning, Albert.
**Albert** (*leaping up*) Morning Sarah! Morning! Morning! (*He switches on the Hoover and resumes work*)

*She switches it off*

**Sarah** Why were you vacuuming the keyhole?
**Albert** You might well ask.
**Sarah** I have. Why were you doing it?
**Albert** What's the question again?
**Sarah** Why were you vacuuming the keyhole?
**Albert** Filthy. Astonishing the dirt and fluff that gathers in our keyholes.

*She passes him and bends down and looks through the keyhole*

**Sarah** There's a piece of fluff in there taking a shower. Why have I caught you spying on a naked woman? (*She puts her handbag and briefcase on a chair*)
**Albert** Because I didn't hear you coming. No ... no ... I didn't mean that. I wanted to see if the shower was working properly.
**Sarah** Who is she anyway?
**Albert** I don't know. When I arrived to tidy up I found her hanging on the geraniums.

*Tom staggers in and leans, panting heavily on the desk. His face is red and sweaty*

*Sarah surveys him for a moment, then undoes her case*

**Sarah** What does he look like? To think I was married to that for twelve years. Can you imagine it, Albert?

**Albert** It's not easy.

**Sarah** No, honestly Tom. You'll have to give it up. You look positively disgusting in that track suit. And your face! All those purple blotches and blood-shot eyes! Actually, you remind me of something . . . I can't think what.

**Albert** (*considering for a moment*) Reminds me of the army.

**Sarah** The army?

**Albert** When I was in the Catering Corps, I once had to shovel up a ton of condemned sausage-meat.

**Sarah** And you shouldn't run on misty days like this, Tom. You know your eyes are going. (*To Albert*) Do you remember that time he had that jog in the fog and ran right off the wharf into the river?

**Albert** (*laughing*) Oh yes. That was a hoot! He got *very* fit that day. He had a swim as well.

**Tom** (*getting his breath*) You wouldn't dare talk about me like that if I could speak. (*He collapses into a chair*) But you're quite right. I can't go on like this . . . burning the candle at both ends.

**Sarah** Which end are you going to give up? (*She picks up her briefcase and crosses to the desk. She opens her briefcase, takes out some papers and files and puts on her glasses*)

*Albert resumes cleaning up*

**Tom** Why are you here?

**Sarah** For the usual reason. As your accountant, I've come to discuss your finances.

**Tom** I knew it was going to be a rotten day.

*The bathroom door opens and Lucy comes out, half-dressed*

**Lucy** Hi!

*She collects her satchel bag and goes back into the bathroom*

**Tom** She's conducting a survey.

**Sarah** Tom, we've been very happily separated for three years now. I'm not in the least interested in your lady friends. My only interest in you is financial. (*She picks up one of the files*)

*Albert switches on the Hoover*

**Tom** Will you stop that dreadful noise and go and make some coffee for my accountant and myself.

**Albert** (*switching off the Hoover*) Milk and sugar?

**Tom** And one of those Eccles cakes you've brought for yourself out of my money.

**Albert** Some of us should give up Eccles cakes. (*He takes the tray and the waste-paper bin with the party debris towards·the kitchen*)

**Tom** He's getting too big for his boots.
**Albert** (*as he exits*) And you're getting too big for your track-suit.

*Albert exits to the kitchen*

**Tom** What? What did he say? He'll have to go. Why are you here? It's not Wednesday.
**Sarah** I'm on my way to Harrods, actually, to buy a bikini. (*She moves behind the sofa*)

*Lucy comes out of the bathroom, dressed*

**Lucy** Excuse me ... could I use your bedroom to put my face on?
**Tom** In there.
**Lucy** Why is it so dim in your bathroom?
**Tom** Because when you're my age you'll prefer to shave in the dark.
**Lucy** (*to Sarah*) Are you the accountant who's also his wife?
**Sarah** Don't let me put you off. We've been apart for years. I no longer cook his dinners, just his books.
**Lucy** When he talked about you last night I didn't imagine you having such a smashing figure.

*Lucy goes into the bedroom*

**Sarah** What a nice girl. How did you manage to pick her up? (*She sits on the arm of the sofa*)
**Tom** You're here as my accountant, so please ... just state your business then go. She wasn't a pick-up. She happens to be a very old friend of mine and she adores me. In fact, *she* says ... and I won't go into further details ... but she says I'm the best lover she's ever had.

*Sarah gives a shriek which she smothers with her hand*

Yes—do laugh. Go ahead. Have a good laugh.
**Sarah** I'm sorry. I didn't realize she was an old friend.
**Tom** Well, she is. A very dear and intimate friend.
**Sarah** What's her name?
**Tom** (*a blank moment*) I'm not going into any more details. State your business, then go.

*Sarah hands him a letter from her file*

What's this?
**Sarah** A letter for you.
**Tom** Who from?
**Sarah** Me.
**Tom** What about?
**Sarah** Read it.

*He examines it warily, holds it up to the light and frowns*

**Tom** It can't be good news. You've never written to me telling me good news.
**Sarah** I wrote you that letter saying I was leaving you.
**Tom** Oh yes! I forgot that. I beg your pardon.

*Albert enters with the coffee on a tray. He places it on the table in front of Sarah*

**Sarah** (*rising*) Thank you, Albert. That was quick. (*She puts the file on the pouffe*)
**Albert** Instant coffee.

*The phone rings. Albert moves to answer it*

**Tom** Take it on the kitchen extension, will you? Whoever it is, I'm out.
**Albert** What time will you be back?
**Tom** After lunch.

*Albert exits to the kitchen*

**Sarah** Go on, open it. (*She takes a cup of coffee from the tray*)

*Tom approaches the letter warily*

**Tom** Why? You're here . . ., tell me what it says. You know I never open my mail before opening time. (*He picks it up carefully*) No, I definitely don't like the look of this letter.
**Sarah** Don't be ridiculous.
**Tom** No, I can tell with letters. This one even feels sinister. (*He takes a bite of Eccles cake*) Oh yes . . . that's one of the crouching ones . . . just waiting for you to open it. (*He goes to open it, but stops*) No . . . there's something up. You visiting me Friday morning . . . neglecting your other clients. You going to Harrods to buy a bikini, in September. And now you write me a letter and deliver it in person. . . . Why?
**Sarah** Because it seemed the most civilized way of breaking the news.
**Tom** What news? (*He spoons sugar into his cup, drinks his coffee and shudders*) Ugh! Albert is the only man I know who can make Turkish coffee out of Nescafe. What news? Don't tell me.
**Sarah** It's a decision I've made.
**Tom** You want to divorce me.
**Sarah** Not especially.
**Tom** Something worse?
**Sarah** In a way.
**Tom** You want to come back to me.
**Sarah** Much more serious than that.
**Tom** You're putting your fees up?
**Sarah** I'm going to Spain for a long rest. It's all in that letter. (*She puts her cup on the pouffe and picks up the file*)
**Tom** You're going on holiday! But that's fine! (*He opens the letter*) You didn't have to write to me about that. Go! It'll do you the world of good. I've got a few pesetas somewhere, and half a bottle of suntan lotion (*He stops as he reads*) What's this? (*He reads*) "Dear Tom, I regret that due to circumstances beyond my control, I can no longer act as your accountant. Yours sincerely, Sarah Davenport, FCA."

*Sarah hands him the file*

What's this?

**Sarah** Photostats of your tax returns for the past eight years which your new accountant will need.

**Tom** And that's me disposed of?

**Sarah** My other clients just got a duplicated letter, but because you are such a fool in money matters, I thought I should come round personally and put you in the picture. I felt I owed you that.

**Tom** Because I'm a financial idiot?

**Sarah** Well, aren't you? For instance, when the BBC paid you twice by mistake there was no necessity for you to refund it to them *with* interest.

**Tom** But that is honesty! It is the only way I know how to live. I don't have many virtues but I am proud of the fact that no man can say I am not as honest as the day is long.

**Sarah** As far as the majority of people are concerned, I am as honest as the day is long.

**Tom** But your days are shorter than mine.

*Lucy enters fully dressed, carrying her bag*

**Lucy** Hi!

**Sarah** Hello again.

*A slight pause while the two look at each other, waiting to be introduced*

Tom, aren't you going to introduce us?

**Tom** Sorry ... permit me. My accountant, Sarah Davenport.

**Sarah** Hello ...

**Tom** My friend ... (*He looks blank for a moment*) ... Lydia.

*She pulls out the elastic top of his trousers again*

**Lucy** Lucy. Lucy Napier.

**Tom** Well I knew it started with an L.

*She lets the elastic go*

*Tom backs into the bathroom*

*Lucy pulls the door shut*

**Lucy** (*jerking her head in his direction*) What a wally! How long were you married to him?

**Sarah** Twelve years. You known him long?

**Lucy** Twelve hours.

**Sarah** A fairly new friend.

**Lucy** He's not really my type.

**Sarah** Tell me, how did you meet him?

**Lucy** These market survey people gave me his name and address 'cos they wanted the opinions of people belonging to B minus.

**Sarah** B minus?

**Lucy** That's his social group. Well, he's an A really, judging by the kit he's got here ... and employing staff.

**Sarah** I'm his accountant. I don't consider myself staff.

**Lucy** No, I mean that wicked old sod who does the cleaning.

**Sarah** So your market survey interview developed into a party, did it?

**Lucy** Yeah ... still, it breaks the monotony. Gawd! I must have had a few last night ... my tattoo is itching. (*She scratches her stomach*) Well, I'd better go home and write up my surveys. Where did I put 'em last night? Oh! Here they are. (*She collects some files and puts them in her copious bag*) I'd better leave him my phone number. If he can't remember my name, he'll never remember my phone number, will he?

**Sarah** Tom?

**Lucy** Yeah. Ah! This'll do. (*She writes the number on Tom's desk*)

**Sarah** I thought you said he was a wally.

**Lucy** He is, but a lot of these fellers who are two strokes to start with often improve when they get to know you.

**Sarah** Two strokes?

**Lucy** You know? Hard to start, splutter a lot, then two strokes and it's over. He might have some potential for me. If he can ever remember my name. (*She puts on a very patched fur coat*) Like me coat? A quid in a jumble sale last week. It's nineteen thirty-nine rabbit.

**Sarah** It's lovely.

**Lucy** Yeah ... I got an eye for bargains. (*She bangs on the bathroom door*) Cheerio, two stroke!

**Tom** (*off*) What? Who's that?

**Lucy** (*smiling at Sarah*) See what I mean? Ta-rah.

**Sarah** (*smiling at her*) Ta-rah!

*Lucy exits*

*Sarah smilingly watches her walk along the catwalk until she is gone*

*Tom comes out of the bathroom wearing trousers and shirt*

**Tom** Where ...? (*He realizes she is gone*) What did she call me?

**Sarah** Better not ask. Now whatever you say won't make any difference. I'm giving up accountancy, and going to live abroad.

**Tom** But why? Give me one good reason.

**Sarah** Joanna Flint.

**Tom** Pardon?

**Sarah** Joanna Flint.

**Tom** I've heard that name quite recently.

**Sarah** She's been your public relations adviser for the past five years.

**Tom** Yes, that name definitely rings a — my *what*?

**Sarah** Public relations adviser.

**Tom** I've never had public relations in my life.

**Sarah** You employed her.

**Tom** I did? No, you've got me mixed up with one of your clients. Flint? Wasn't that the wrong number? That chap from the Inland Revenue who rang here? It must have been 'cos I've never heard of her in my life. In fact, I thought it might be that Lydia Naples girl.

**Sarah** Lucy Napier.

**Tom** That's right. No, really Sarah . . . you're confused. The sooner you get away on that holiday the better.

**Sarah** Tom, will you listen to me . . .?

**Tom** It's overwork . . . stress——

**Sarah** Will you shut up and listen.

**Tom** Sarah, you're upset——

**Sarah** Shut up!

**Tom** You don't have to shout.

**Sarah** (*quietly*) I do have to shout. It's the only way I could ever have a conversation with you.

**Tom** That's better.

**Sarah** Be quiet. Sit still and listen.

*Tom obediently sits*

Thank you.

**Tom** Don't mention it.

**Sarah** Shut up!

**Tom** Sorry.

**Sarah** Now . . . this lady. Joanna Flint. You have employed her for five years. Each year you have paid her a fee for PR consultation and advice.

*Tom puts his hand up*

**Tom** Permission to speak.

**Sarah** Later.

**Tom** But I've never even met the bloody woman!

**Sarah** That is completely beside the point. Miss Flint has appeared regularly in your life since nineteen seventy-eight.

**Tom** Appeared where?

**Sarah** On your tax return.

*He stares at her*

She has been an annual deduction . . . an item under business expenses, approved and accepted by the Inland Revenue. She has, over this time, saved you a large amount of tax . . . even though, as you may have gathered by now . . . Miss Flint does not exist.

*Tom remains staring at her, open-mouthed*

At least, not outside the pages of your annual return. The trouble is . . . I think HM Tax is on to her. Will you please say something.

**Tom** You told me not to.

**Sarah** Until I'd finished. I've finished.

**Tom** You made her up?

**Sarah** Yes.

**Tom** And the Revenue's rumbled her?

**Sarah** I think so. Yes, I definitely think they're after her. You see, she hasn't paid any tax on the money you paid her.

**Tom** How could she? You say she doesn't exist.

**Sarah** Don't split hairs Tom. If you claim tax relief for a figment of the imagination, that figment has to pay tax just like everyone else.

**Tom** (*baffled*) How? With what? A figment of the imagination cheque?

**Sarah** Please, Tom ... be serious.

**Tom** I've never been more serious. Are you telling me that for the past five years I have swindled the tax people?

**Sarah** Inadvertently. You didn't know it.

**Tom** I didn't.

**Sarah** I know. It is totally my fault, Tom. I take all the blame.

**Tom** Sarah, I am just a humble doctor of botany who earns a simple crust as a compère on a gardening chat show. You know how peculiar I am about money. I am incapable of adding up a restaurant bill. Waiters see me coming a mile off. So ... will you please start from the beginning. Did I employ her when I was doing research on the viral diseases of root vegetables at Newcastle University?

**Sarah** No. There was no need ... You were nothing then. Just another botanist with a Ph.D. It was when you left to become technical adviser on that gardening programme on the telly ... and wrote that book *Living Off Your Window Box* and you got all those royalties.

**Tom** How much have I paid her?

**Sarah** Over five years ... in round figures ... thirty thousand pounds.

**Tom** Sarah ... this is totally immoral. I never asked you ... I never wanted ... I've always been happy about paying my tax.

**Sarah** Because you paid so little. Anyway, Miss Flint is in dead trouble.

**Tom** What about me? All those fraudulent returns I've been sending ...

**Sarah** Yes, well ... frankly, we are *all* in trouble.

**Tom** Which is why you are running off to Spain and deserting me. While I'm in the nick, you'll be getting a suntan. I am a totally innocent party. I never asked you to invent this dreadful woman.

**Sarah** I know. It's just a little favour I did for you. The thing is, you are legally responsible for your own tax returns.

**Tom** But I never asked you ...

**Sarah** You signed your tax returns.

**Tom** But you know I never *read* them! I just sign them where you mark with a cross! This is outrageous, Sarah ... you've gone too far ... No-one minds a *bit* of a fiddle. We all try to pay as little tax as we can. Who hasn't walked past the Customs at Dover over our limit on the Duty Frees? But a crafty bottle of Gordons is one thing ... me paying Miss Flint thirty thousand pounds is another!

*Albert enters from the kitchen*

**Albert** We're out of Brillo pads!

**Tom** Brillo pads?! Don't talk to me about Brillo pads.

**Albert** And Ajax. We're out of that too.

**Tom** I am not in the slightest interested in your domestic problems. Do you know what Sarah has done to me?

**Albert** Yes, I've been listening.

**Tom** Sarah has turned me into an even bigger crook than you.

**Albert** I know. It must have taken some doing, Sarah.

**Tom** And that phone call! They must be on to me already! That call from the Inland Revenue wasn't a wrong number after all. They really believe that Miss Flint is here working for me.

**Sarah** And I'm afraid they're beginning to close in.

**Tom** You mean my arrest is imminent?

**Albert** They can't do that to you. You've got seven programmes on pot plants to do for Capital Radio.

**Tom** The disgrace will ruin me Sarah!

**Albert** It will. He's a public figure. He's got two lines in *Who Was Who*.

**Tom** I've got two lines in *Who's Who*.

**Albert** I'm talking about next year ... when you're in Wormwood Scrubs.

**Tom** Albert! Will you kindly belt up!

**Sarah** Look — let's not get excited.

**Albert** She does tend to get hysterical these days.

**Sarah** I'm not hysterical at all, Albert.

**Albert** No, I meant him.

**Tom** What am I going to do? What the hell am I going to do?

**Albert** Well, for a start, I'd listen to what Sarah has to say. She didn't come all this way to pass the time of day.

**Sarah** Thank you, Albert.

**Tom** (*to Sarah*) You mean you know how to get out of this?

**Sarah** I think so.

**Tom** How?

**Sarah** Well, as soon as I settle in Spain, you're going to get a letter from Joanna Flint. She'll write to say she is in a bit of financial trouble, and is not coming back ... so she's sorry she can no longer work for you.

**Tom** And then what?

**Sarah** You send her a letter saying how annoyed and disappointed you are——

**Albert** Be sure to keep a carbon.

**Sarah** She'll write back. A short, curt note, informing you that her life is her own business ... and kindly don't bother her again.

**Albert** Clever girl, Sarah.

**Tom** But will the tax people believe it?

**Sarah** They'll have to.

**Tom** I suppose it might work.

**Albert** Oh, I nearly forgot. A pal of yours rang. A bloke called Dodds. Gilbert Dodds.

**Tom** Dodds? That name's familiar.

**Albert** Well, he wanted——

**Sarah** He's the inspector who's causing all this trouble.

**Albert** Inspector?

**Tom** Of course, he phoned this morning. (*To Albert*) What did he say? Albert?

**Albert** That he wanted to see you.

**Tom** What did you say?

**Albert** As instructed, that you were out. And that you'd be back after lunch. So he's calling at two.

**Tom** (*to Albert*) You've invited him round here? *Invited* him to nick me!

**Albert** Well I didn't know. I thought he was that new publisher of yours. He said that you and him had some mutual interests.

**Tom** We have! He's interested in sending me to prison . . . I'm interested in staying out! What do I say to him, Sarah? Help me! If I'm up at the Old Bailey for fraud, I'm finished. They'll never have me on "Gardeners' Questions" again!

**Albert** You might get on "Call My Bluff".

*Tom glares*

No . . . no . . . I didn't mean that. (*He slaps his hand*) Be serious, Albert.

**Tom** As a scientific horticulturist, I'll never be taken seriously again. All the years I spent developing a potato which would grow where they've never grown before. I've got a variety named after me. The Lambert Majestic! I've written nine papers and two books on potatoes. If this gets out, you can see the headlines . . .

**Albert** Yeah. "Potato Doctor gets the Blight."

**Tom** Exactly.

**Albert** "Potato doctor lands in liquid manure."

**Tom** That's right.

**Albert** "Potato doctor gets his chips."

**Tom** I know.

**Albert** "Potato———"

**Tom** (*shouting*) Will you shut up!

*Pause*

**Albert** In fact, you'll be lucky to get a job cleaning Percy Thrower's gumboots!

*Tom grabs Albert by the neck*

**Tom** Will you stop undermining me!

**Albert** Careful with my shirt. I only pinched it last week from the launderette.

**Sarah** Tom, don't get so excited. It's just an enquiry, a routine enquiry, not a raid by the Sweeney. (*A beat*) Mind you, it is a bit unusual . . .

**Tom** What do you mean . . . "unusual"?

**Sarah** An inspector actually calling . . . they do call, of course, but only in more serious cases.

**Tom** Serious . . .?

**Sarah** Anyway, don't let's jump the gun. If we just keep our heads . . .

**Tom** You're right. Anyway, thank God you'll be here to answer all his questions.

**Sarah** No, I'll be at Harrods getting my summer clothes.

**Tom** What! You can't do that. You can't just leave me here in the . . . the . . .

**Albert** Compost.

**Tom** That's right . . . thank you. You can't just leave me in that, while you're parading up and down Harrods in a bikini!

**Sarah** If I was here, then he would be suspicious. You — flanked by your accountant — he'd know immediately something was up.

*Tom tries to speak*

No, keep quiet and listen. All you have to say is yes, Miss Flint has worked for you . . . in fact, man to man, you might tell him there's been a bit going on after work. But she's suddenly left . . . and you can't contact her. (*She collects her handbag*)

**Tom** What was her last address?

**Sarah** (*blankly*) Er . . .

**Sarah** She must've had one.

**Sarah** Er . . .

**Tom** It'll be the first question he'll ask.

**Sarah** I expect so.

**Tom** So where did she live . . . Downing Street?

*A slightly awkward pause*

**Albert** Might I make a suggestion?

**Sarah** Please, Albert.

**Albert** Miss Flint, until a short time ago, was staying here.

*They both look at him*

I believe, if called upon, I could testify to that. Rather untidy in her ways. Suddenly, one day, to my great relief, she moved out . . . since when you've been trying to find her.

**Sarah** (*to Albert*) I think it's a wonderful idea. At least it'll stall Mr Dodds for the moment. And then once I'm in Spain . . .

**Albert** The exchange of letters can begin.

**Sarah** You are lovely, Albert.

**Albert** Thank you, Sarah. I've always felt the same about you.

**Tom** It'll never work.

*Sarah collects her briefcase*

**Sarah** It must. It will . . . if you're calm and composed. I'll come back after he's gone. Trust me, Tom.

**Albert** I'd suggest a phone call, from the box on the corner, just to make sure he has gone.

**Sarah** You're quite right, Albert. (*Concerned*) Tom, do relax. It's for the best. Trust me.

*Sarah moves to the door and exits*

**Tom** (*following her to the door*) I have trusted you. (*Calling after her*) I trusted you for years . . . (*He comes back into the room*) Unbelievable! She drops me right in it, then walks out. What do I tell Dodds? If I say Miss Flint doesn't exist, I'm admitting that I've sent in false tax returns. If I say I know Miss Flint very well because she has been my public relations consultant for five years, why don't I know where she lives? What am I going to do, Albert?

**Albert** How about a spot of brandy? That might help. (*He goes to the sideboard*)

**Tom** What? No. I must keep a clear head.

**Albert** Come on. Do you good. (*He pours two large brandies*) Although the sun is barely half-way to the yard-arm, I'm tempted to join you.

**Tom** Right.

*Albert hands one glass to Tom, and taking the other swallows half a glassful*

**Albert** I must say you always stock good brandy. (*Thoughtfully*) That's an alternative, I suppose.

**Tom** What is?

**Albert** We could get so pissed that you can't even talk to him.

**Tom** Why should both of us get pissed?

**Albert** Well, I'm assuming you'd rather not drink alone.

**Tom** You drink. I've got to stay sober.

**Albert** That's very civil of you. (*He downs his brandy, and takes Tom's untouched glass*)

**Tom** I've got to stay calm and controlled. Razor-sharp, ready for anything. It'll be a battle of wits ... and I think I'm going to lose.

*He props his chin in his hands, staring and miserable. Albert sips the other brandy as he sits beside him*

**Albert** I once knew a girl called Flint. In summer season at Paignton.

**Tom** I wish she was here now.

**Albert** I doubt it. Not if you'd seen her. She was voted the girl you'd least like to be left alone on the pier with, when the lights went out. (*He takes another sip of brandy*) Here. Hang about! ... That might be the answer.

**Tom** What might be?

**Albert** What you just said. That you wished she was here now.

**Tom** I don't follow.

**Albert** Look, what you need is a Miss Flint — here — this afternoon. She sweeps in — answers a few questions put by the tax man — promises to come and see him to sort things out — then disappears — scarpers.

**Tom** (*thoughtfully*) And writes to me from Spain with rude messages for the Inland Revenue. It might work.

**Albert** It's worth a try. Where's your address book?

*Tom rises and finds his address book, and starts to thumb through it*

**Tom** Let's see ... Helena? No, she's a twit. Marigold? Mmmm ... ahh, Karen ... she's game for anything.

*He goes to the phone and dials a number. During this Albert refills his glass*

Karen? Hello, my darling. ... No, it isn't George ... it's Tom ... Tom Lambert. ... Yes, it was lovely, wasn't it ... we must do it again soon. Look, Karen ... I wonder if you could do me a great favour ... are you free this afternoon? . . . Marvellous. Could you come across . . . I mean come round . . . bit of a gag . . . there's an inspector from the tax department descending on me at two . . . and, just for fun, I want you to impersonate a lady who owes a few years' back taxes . . . that's all you have to do and . . . Karen? (*He looks at the receiver*) The rotten coward. She hung up.

*The Lights fade to a Black-out*

<br>

SCENE 2

*The same. That afternoon, about 1.45 p.m.*

*Albert is spraying the plants and weaving about, drunk*

*Tom appears on the catwalk and hurries towards the front door. He opens it and enters*

**Tom**  God, I've been everywhere. I've asked everyone. (*He takes his address book from his pocket and tosses it disconsolately on the desk*) Wouldn't you think one — just one — of all those ladies I've wined and dined, would offer to help. But no . . . at the first mention of the Inland Revenue they all turn to jelly — or water — or whatever people turn to. It's nearly two o'clock and I need a brandy.

**Albert**  Good. I hope you bought another bottle.

**Tom**  (*picking up the empty bottle*) You've drunk it!

**Albert**  I do find, as I get older, the bottles tend to get smaller. It may be something to do with the metric system, or the Common Market. (*He puts the plant spray on the workbench, comes down the steps, takes his brandy glass, collects the other glass and takes the empty bottle from Tom*)

**Tom**  You realize, at any moment, that tax inspector is going to arrive?

**Albert**  (*blankly*) Eh?

**Tom**  Doesn't the name Dodds ring a bell?

**Albert**  In my present state, I can hear bells without help from anybody.

*He takes the glasses and bottle and exits into the kitchen*

*Tom sighs. He paces about. Stops. Starts to rehearse what to say*

**Tom**  Now look here, Dodds . . . (*He stops*) . . . no . . . (*He tries another tone*) My dear Mr Dodds . . . (*He pauses*) Interesting name, Dodds. Would you be related to the Devonshire Dodds?

*Albert hurriedly reappears from the kitchen. Alarmed*

**Albert**  (*collecting his mac and cap from the cupboard*) I'm off.

**Tom**  Where?

**Albert**  (*evasively*) I . . . have another engagement.

**Tom**  But you're supposed to stay here and tell the inspector you know Miss Flint. How she's gone away without a forwarding address. You promised.

**Albert** I did. But since then I've taken advice.

**Tom** Advice? From who?

**Albert** Well, I phoned Vera and she says it'd be better for me to keep a low profile with the Inland Revenue. You see, as far as they are concerned, I haven't existed since April the tenth nineteen sixty-eight.

**Tom** You mean you haven't paid tax since then?

**Albert** How can I put it? No. Then I spoke to my common-law missis. And Dora said she saw no point in me coming face to face with a tax inspector if it could be decently avoided.

**Tom** So the tax people are looking for you too?

**Albert** Well, I'm not in the same league as your clever self – even so . . . as Madelaine says . . .

**Tom** Madelaine?

**Albert** You know? My new girl friend – the one who demonstrates in Selfridges. I phoned her too, and she thought you'd be much happier if I left you alone to sort it out for yourself . . .

**Tom** Go on then you rat! You treacherous, weak-kneed, disloyal . . . desert the sinking ship!

**Albert** I'll be back to clean it on Friday – if it's still afloat. (*He stops at the door*) Oh! I should hide that Picasso if I were you. I know it's not one of his best paintings, but it might get *them* over-excited.

*Albert exits hurriedly*

*Tom hurries to the Picasso and takes it down from the wall. There is a picture light fixed to the wall above it and that and the hook plus the darker colour on the wall make it obvious a painting has been recently removed. He worries about this for a moment while holding the painting, then decides he can do nothing about it. He comes downstage looking for a place to hide the Picasso. He tries putting it under the sofa, then decides against this. Finally, he wraps it in a green plastic bag and places it down on the table amongst his laboratory equipment. He moves a few specimen jars containing plants so that it does not look as if the bag has recently been placed there*

*In the background Albert hurries back, and fumbles for his key*

*Tom sees him, reacts, and hurries to let him in, leaving the door ajar*

He's here!

**Tom** What?

**Albert** I heard a car pull up.

**Tom** What did he look like?

**Albert** I didn't stop to see. I need to sit down. I think I may have a heart attack.

**Tom** Well, have it in the bedroom. You're all I need, flipping your lid and upsetting my equilibrium.

*He pushes Albert in the direction of the bedroom*

**Albert** What about my equal . . . what about that?

*Albert exits through the archway towards the bedroom*

*Tom tries to psych himself up for the encounter. He nervously shifts a few objects around the wrapped Picasso, then grabs a book and sits down in a chair, attempting to give the impression of a man relaxed*

> *A moment passes, and Sarah appears along the catwalk, carrying her briefcase and handbag. She hurriedly enters the door, which has been left ajar. As she closes it:*

**Tom** (*without turning, as casually as he can*) Anyone there?
**Sarah** (*anxious and out of breath*) Tom . . .

*He reacts and jumps up*

**Tom** What the hell are you doing?
**Sarah** I had to come back.
**Tom** Thank God!

*His surprise changes to buoyant relief, as he puts an arm around her and kisses her on the cheek. Sarah is hardly aware of it, possessed of an urgency he fails to notice*

**Sarah** He hasn't been? Mr Dodds?
**Tom** He hasn't been. We thought you were him. (*He calls*) Albert!
**Sarah** I had to try and make it, before he got here. (*She puts her briefcase down*)
**Tom** You cut it a bit fine, my darling, but you're welcome.

> *Albert emerges from the direction of the bedroom*

**Albert** You certainly are.
**Tom** I've never been more pleased to see anyone in my life. I should've had more faith.
**Sarah** (*confused*) In what?
**Tom** In you. Your loyalty, your . . . your honesty.
**Albert** You should've.
**Tom** (*to Albert*) Go on, now's your chance. Slope off.
**Albert** I think I will, if no-one minds.

*No-one even notices as he makes his way to the front door*

**Sarah** Tom, listen to me . . .
**Tom** No, let me say this. We've had our ups and downs, you and me . . . but you came back when it mattered. You don't know how much this means, what confidence it gives me. We'll front him together.
**Sarah** No we won't.
**Tom** I'll hold your hand while you answer his——What do you mean we won't?
**Sarah** We've decided that. It's too obvious if I'm here as your accountant.
**Tom** Then why are you here? Why'd you come back?
**Sarah** Because there's something I didn't tell you . . . and I think you should know.
**Tom** Something else?
**Sarah** Yes.

*Albert has been standing upstage, unnoticed at the front door, his expression changing with the news, from one of contentment to alarm*

**Albert** (*a* non-sequitur *announcement*) Well, I think I will, then. While the going's good.

*He exits along the catwalk*

*Neither of them pays the slightest attention*

**Tom** Something you omitted to mention?
**Sarah** Deliberately omitted.
**Tom** Why?
**Sarah** I thought it might upset you.
**Tom** And now you want to tell me?
**Sarah** Yes.
**Tom** Before Didds gets here?
**Sarah** His name is Dodds. Gilbert P. Dodds. Tom!
**Tom** Sarah ... please don't tell me.
**Sarah** I must. It's important.
**Tom** Important good or important bad?
**Sarah** Well, it depends.
**Tom** I definitely don't want to hear it.
**Sarah** I raced back here. I was in Harrods, and I thought, it's not fair, it just isn't right leaving him in ignorance ...
**Tom** I was ignorant yesterday. It was wonderful.
**Sarah** Please, Tom. I have to explain before he gets here. What's the time? How long have we got?
**Tom** (*looking at his watch*) Four minutes if he's punctual.
**Sarah** I don't exactly know how to begin.
**Tom** Maybe ten minutes if he's late.
**Sarah** It's very difficult. It's not something you can say just like that.
**Tom** Then don't say it at all.
**Sarah** But I must.

*Albert hurries back along the catwalk, and in the front door which he leaves ajar*

**Albert** He's here!
**Tom** Albert!
**Albert** It's definitely him this time. Bit thin on top, an old Mini and a briefcase.

*Albert hurries across and disappears in the direction of the bedroom*

*Sarah picks up her briefcase*

**Tom** Quick, tell me. What is it I should know?
**Sarah** There's not time. Where will I go?
**Tom** In there with Albert.

*She heads off in the direction of the bedroom*

*Tom suddenly notices her handbag left behind and throws it after her. He flops down in the chair and grabs up the book, reading it upside down*

> *As he does so, in the background on the catwalk Mr Dodds appears. He looks around him at the view, then in through the picture windows. Mr Dodds is a man of indeterminate age, but probably in his fifties. His suit is well worn and he carries a shabby leather briefcase. He looks, on first impression, like a rather unsuccessful private detective. He comes and stops by the front door, realizing it is open. He taps on the glass, remains there*

*Tom continues to read the book upside down*

**Dodds** (*diffidently*) Anybody home?

*Tom gets up*

**Tom** Ahhh!

**Dodds** Good-afternoon. It's Mr Lambert of course. May I say at once how much my wife and I enjoy your programmes?

**Tom** (*relaxing immediately*) Oh! Thank you very much.

**Dodds** My name is Dodds ... Gilbert Dodds. Inland Revenue. My identification. (*He produces an identification wallet and hands it to Tom*) I do hope it's not too inconvenient my popping in like this at such short notice, but I spoke to your gentleman cleaner a little earlier.

**Tom** Er ... quite.

**Dodds** I won't take long, Mr Lambert. I know you're a very busy man, but if you could spare me a few moments, I'd be so grateful.

**Tom** Yes, of course. Come in.

**Dodds** How very kind of you! Especially as the——

*Dodds enters and Tom shuts the door*

—— business I've come about doesn't concern you at all ...

**Tom** (*brightening*) It doesn't? (*He hands back the wallet*) Splendid! – I mean, thank you.

**Dodds** Not directly. It's just that I'm trying to locate the whereabouts of someone who performed some professional services for you.

**Tom** Oh yes?

**Dodds** A lady.

**Tom** Oh yes? Which one? There's Mrs Kingsley who types my TV scripts. She lives at twenty-seven A Streatham High Street, over the dry cleaners. Then there's Barbara Webster, my part-time secretary. She comes in every Monday and deals with my correspondence ... She lives at six Jubilee Terrace, East Molesey.

**Dodds** No, I am not interested in any of those ladies.

**Tom** You're not?

**Dodds** No ... it's the lady who is your public relations consultant ... Miss Joanna Flint.

**Tom** Ah!

**Dodds** You do, of course, know about this lady?

**Tom** Yes ... yes indeed.

**Dodds** I'm delighted to hear it, because no-one at the Inland Revenue does
... and she owes us rather a lot of tax.

**Tom** That a fact?

**Dodds** We've used all the usual methods for tracking her down and, as you
can imagine, the Inland Revenue are rather good at tracking people down.

**Tom** Yes. I know. Naturally. I can imagine.

**Dodds** But we have drawn a total blank with her. Have *you* any idea where
she might be found, Mr Lambert?

**Tom** No.

**Dodds** Oh dear! Oh goodness me. I had such high hopes of you, Mr Lambert.

**Tom** I'm sorry to be a let-down, Mr Dodds.

**Dodds** There are fourteen hundred and thirty-eight Flints listed in various
phone directories and electoral rolls in this country ... we've tried them all
without success. She is not known or related to any of them.

**Tom** There are no Joanna Flints?

**Dodds** Oh yes! There are three, as a matter of fact, but none of them is the
Joanna Flint we're looking for. There's an eighty-seven-year-old Joanna
Flint who is a recluse in Chorlton-cum-Hardy, and a highly respectable
Joanna Flint who is a dentist in Droitwich.

**Tom** What about the third Joanna Flint?

**Dodds** I've had to eliminate her as well.

**Tom** Why?

**Dodds** Well, I don't know if it was the result of our various representatives
knocking on her door ... but she has become John Flint.

**Tom** It seems rather a drastic way of avoiding paying tax.

**Dodds** Quite. I'd much rather have a few pounds deducted from my pay
packet ...

**Tom** Than a few deductions from my ...

**Dodds** Quite. Could she have gone abroad you think?

**Tom** Er—would that ... er ... help your enquiries?

**Dodds** Hardly. It would put the kibosh on them completely.

**Tom** Well, her parents live abroad.

**Dodds** Where?

**Tom** Zimbabwe.

**Dodds** Zimbabwe. Yes, I see. Might I sit down for a moment, Mr Lambert
and make a note of that?

**Tom** Please do.

**Dodds** Awfully kind of you. (*He sits and arranges his papers and makes odd
notes as he sifts through his documents*) Some people don't like me to do
that.

**Tom** Make notes?

**Dodds** Sit down. You're within your rights to refuse me a chair you know.

**Tom** I didn't know.

**Dodds** Very few do. I like to play fair. Inform a citizen of his rights and
privileges. They're all here in this booklet published by the HMSO Tax
Office sixteen C stroke seven. Tells you all the rights you have in dealing
with tax officers in any situation. (*Offering Tom a booklet*) Do take it. I've
plenty of spares.

**Tom** (*gingerly taking the booklet*) But do I need it? I mean ... I'm not in a situation, am I?

**Dodds** (*smiling at him*) Not at this point of time Mr Lambert ... no. (*He writes*) "Parents live in Zimbabwe." Is Miss Flint a coloured lady?

**Tom** Coloured?

**Dodds** I'm not being racist, merely seeking clarification.

**Tom** Does it affect your enquiries?

**Dodds** Not in the least.

**Tom** Well, she's not then.

**Dodds** (*writing*) No ... English Law is very particular when it comes to invasion of privacy. For instance, not only needn't you offer me a seat, but if your books are behind a locked door, you're not obliged to give me the key. Or if I should bring in a photocopy machine, you're entitled to stop me using your electricity.

**Tom** What happens then?

**Dodds** Well, then I'd get a court order which would give me a power of entry day or night, and complete access to all your papers, books, documents ... everything you own, in fact.

**Tom** It won't come to that, surely? (*He laughs*)

**Dodds** Goodness me, no. Why should it? You haven't made a misleading, inaccurate, false or fraudulent statement to the Inland Revenue, have you, Mr Lambert?

**Tom** No ... no ... not me.

**Dodds** You wouldn't ... not someone such as yourself in the public eye. The publicity which would result from a successful prosecution of such as yourself would be ruinous.

**Tom** That's right.

**Dodds** Just imagine what your viewers would think of you? I mean, those who watch your gardening programme on BBC every Sunday morning. It really is a pleasure to meet you in person, Mr Lambert. I've never seen potting begonias in a living room beforehand. You have the gift of making things so simple, Mr Lambert.

**Tom** Thank you.

**Dodds** And meeting you in the flesh today ... it's odd. I feel I know you so well.

**Tom** Oh! (*A beat*) Nice.

**Dodds** And while I'm here ... I hope you won't mind my asking you, but I'm having a lot of trouble with my leeks.

**Tom** Leeks? Not in my field.

**Dodds** (*laughing*) That's rather humorous, Mr Lambert.

**Tom** It is? Er ... well, germination can be a problem.

**Dodds** But that's it. You've hit it! I sow the seeds at the right time, in the right soil, but so few come up. Am I on the wrong side of Tulse Hill? I face east, you know.

**Tom** You could try soaking the seeds in warm water for twelve hours.

**Dodds** Soak the seeds in warm water? What an excellent tip. I'll write that down. My wife does so enjoy a good leek.

**Tom** Oh ... (*He pauses*) Nice.

**Dodds** But to business. Mustn't waste the tax-payers' time ... particularly
your time Mr Lambert ... for I see by my records that for the past five
years you have been in the top five per cent of wage-earners.

**Tom** Really?

**Dodds** Although it has to be said that you haven't been among the top five
per cent tax-payers.

**Tom** I haven't?

**Dodds** Anyway, it is not you I've come to investigate but (*He consults his file*)
Mr Henry Morgan.

**Tom** Henry Morgan?

**Dodds** What? No ... no ... I've just finished with him. So sorry ... (*He
shuffles his files*)

**Tom** What happened to him?

**Dodds** He started a three-year term of imprisonment yesterday. (*He sorts
through papers*) Ah, yes ... Miss Joanna Flint. Now, according to your tax
returns, you have paid her approximately thirty thousand pounds over the
past five years in the way of fees for her consultancy services.

**Tom** If you say so, Mr Dodds.

**Dodds** No, you have said so in your various tax returns and these sums have
been accepted and agreed by the Inland Revenue.

**Tom** Yes ... well ... I'm not sure of the exact figure.

**Dodds** It's thirty thousand one hundred and five pounds.

**Tom** Right.

**Dodds** But to date, we have not had from her one penny in tax. A most
elusive lady.

**Tom** Really?

**Dodds** Yet she is not elusive to you?

**Tom** Elusive?

**Dodds** What I mean is, you seem to be in constant touch with her. Last year
alone you paid her ten thousand pounds in fees, for instance.

**Tom** I *was* in touch with her then.

**Dodds** But now?

**Tom** No ... I don't even know her present address.

**Dodds** But doubtless you know her previous address?

**Tom** To be quite frank with you, Mr Dodds ... Joanna was living here for
some time.

**Dodds** I see.

**Tom** But no longer.

**Dodds** She didn't leave a forwarding address?

**Tom** No — because ... to be brutally frank ... she didn't want me to find her.

**Dodds** Ah!

**Tom** You see Mr Dodds, although my relationship with Miss Flint *was*
purely professional for some years, it became personal ... till we had a row.

**Dodds** She left in a huff?

**Tom** Exactly.

**Dodds** This was?

**Tom** Three months ago.

**Dodds** And she has not been in touch since?

**Tom** Afraid not.

**Dodds** I see. Yes. A picture is beginning to emerge. So for some time she lived here in a dual capacity?

**Tom** Dual?

**Dodds** As your public relations consultant and as your common-law wife?

**Tom** Well, not quite. I'm married already.

**Dodds** Yes indeed — to a lady who is also your accountant. I used the expression "common-law wife" to signify what it usually signifies these days.

**Tom** What's that?

**Dodds** A bit on the side — excuse my indelicacy.

**Tom** No . . . no . . . that's the truth . . . we did cohabit for a time.

**Dodds** But she's now left and disappeared without trace?

**Tom** That's it . . . the total thing in a nutshell.

**Dodds** Well it's not totally in the nutshell. There are a few odds and ends still outside the nutshell. For instance, why did you not remember her when I rang you this morning?

*Tom stares — glassily*

Your actual words were . . . (*He reads from his notebook*) "No, I've never even heard of Miss Flint."

**Tom** Me? I said that?

**Dodds** Yes. You said your name was Lambert then made that statement.

**Tom** Yes, I'm sure I said I was Lambert. That is the truth. That is my name, but it'd be ridiculous for me to make a statement like that. No, no . . . you must have misunderstood. I know Miss Flint well . . . very well.

*Dodds promptly produces a mini tape-recorder from his briefcase. He stabs a button and Tom's voice is heard*

**Tom's Voice** No, I've never even heard of Miss Flint.

*Dodds clicks it off and looks at him*

**Tom** (*a beat*) Yes, that's me. Yes, I'll be quite honest with you. That is me.

**Dodds** It's also on the master tape at the office.

**Tom** Oh, good. You've got all the latest gadgets down there then? Yes, that is definitely me. No point in denying it.

**Dodds** (*politely*) Would you like to explain it?

**Tom** I would. I'd like to very much. (*A pause. He stares blankly*) Yes — well . . . I said that because . . . well, er . . . just the other . . . this morning . . . (*His voice trails over into gibberish*)

**Dodds** Pardon me?

**Tom** I said . . . would you like a coffee?

**Dodds** No thank you. Why did you deny knowing Miss Flint?

**Tom** There is a reason why my two statements were totally contradictory, but it is embarrassing, and somewhat personal.

**Dodds** Nothing embarrasses us, sir. Matrimony, polygamy, incest, perversion, masochism, sadism, bondage, sado-masochism . . . the Inland Revenue is only embarrassed by one word . . . evasion.

**Tom** Quite. I am definitely not being evasive ... reluctant maybe.

**Dodds** I must ask you to give me an answer, sir. Why, when I rang this morning did you deny all knowledge of the lady who has been your public relations consultant for the past five years?

**Tom** Well, come on, Mr Dodds. Why do you think?

**Dodds** Would I ask if I knew?

**Tom** You're a man of the world.

**Dodds** One hopes so.

**Tom** Well, you could have been anyone ringing up, claiming to be Mr Dodds of the tax office and asking for Miss Flint.

**Dodds** You suspected I might be someone else?

**Tom** Yes.

**Dodds** And you were protecting her?

**Tom** Yes.

**Dodds** From whom?

**Tom** (*a beat*) Her husband.

**Dodds** Ah! So Miss Flint is married?

**Tom** (*hesitating*) Er ... nn ... yes!

**Dodds** Excellent. (*He makes a note*) Her married name is ...?

**Tom** She never talked about it. She hated him.

**Dodds** I see. She did not want her husband to find out that you and she were cohabiting at this address?

**Tom** Exactly. Or rather ... *had* been cohabiting. Had been. Past tense. I didn't want him to find out anything.

**Dodds** (*writing*) Yes ... well, I am getting a much clearer picture of Miss Flint now. I'll be frank with you, Mr Lambert, when I arrived, I had a strong suspicion that Miss Flint did not exist.

**Tom** Didn't exist! She broke my heart when she walked out on me.

**Dodds** I see. I take it that all the sums you paid her were purely for her services as your public relations consultant?

**Tom** What else?

**Dodds** I recently had a case of a gentleman who manufactured ladies swimwear and every time he visited this brothel in Curzon Street he paid by Barclaycard and then claimed it as a bona-fide business expense.

**Tom** How?

**Dodds** By stating that she supplied him with all his elastic.

**Tom** (*outraged*) And you are suggesting that I paid Miss Flint for sexual favours?

**Dodds** Not at all, sir. I am merely acquainting you with the Revenue's position in these matters ... out of interest. I was not implying that that was your situation with Miss Flint.

**Tom** I see.

**Dodds** If I have inadvertently caused you any offence, sir, I apologize without reserve.

**Tom** Quite all right. Let's forget it.

**Dodds** Mind you, even tarts have to pay tax.

**Tom** Isn't it a crime to live off immoral earnings?

**Dodds** Not with us. Of course we don't lean on them too heavily. We don't want them to wear themselves out. The art of taxation, you see Mr Lambert, consists in plucking the goose, so as to obtain the largest amount of feathers with the least amount of hissing. Anyway, sir, if you'd like to give me Miss Flint's telephone number, I won't delay you any more.

**Tom** Her phone number? I told you. I've no idea where she has gone, where she is living, and I haven't the remotest idea of her phone number.

**Dodds** Well, give me her old number and I'll take it from there.

**Tom** It was ex-directory.

**Dodds** Mr Lambert, I realize you're trying to protect the lady, but I am obliged to trace her. Just give me her number and I won't trouble you further.

**Tom** Her old number?

**Dodds** Yes, it must be in your phone book. She was with you for five years.

**Tom** Er ... er ... I'll have to consult my ... it's in the bedroom.

*Tom goes into the bedroom*

*Dodds rises and looks round the room. He studies the space that the Picasso occupied. Then his attention is taken by the phone number Lucy wrote on the desk. He moves from there to the laboratory table. He examines the plants and apparatus*

*Tom comes out. He reacts nervously as he sees Dodds looking at the green plastic bag*

Mr Dodds, I don't think I can help you further. You have no authority in law to force me into divulging private information about a third party.

**Dodds** That's perfectly true, Mr Lambert. At this stage I do not.

**Tom** As I told you before, I am very fond of Miss Flint, and though I have lost contact with her at the moment ... although we are not, in fact, speaking to each other, I would not like to be the one who gets her into trouble.

**Dodds** (*blandly*) Quite understandable, Mr Lambert. I just hoped you might co-operate. Never mind, we have other avenues.

**Tom** Look, Mr Dodds, aren't you going a bit over the top on this? I mean, I assume she owes a bit of tax?

**Dodds** Five years of tax.

**Tom** Well, that's careless of her, but after all——

**Dodds** We can't have it, you know. There's too much of it going on. I respect you for trying to shield the lady. If I ever found myself in your situation I hope I would protect Mrs Dodds as chivalrously. (*He considers*) Well, certainly I would have in the early days of our marriage ...

**Tom** I swear to you, Mr Dodds, that I am speaking the truth when I say I do not know Miss Flint's phone number. Never have I told the truth as I'm telling it now. I am prepared to swear on a stack of bibles a mile high ... I do not know Miss Flint's phone number.

**Dodds** Is she beautiful, Mr Lambert?

**Tom** Well ... yes ... she's beautiful to me.

**Dodds** What age?

**Tom** Oh ... you know ...

**Dodds** Twenty-five? Thirty-five? Forty-five?

**Tom** You know ... average age. She's never actually told me her exact age.

**Dodds** How charming. Mrs Dodds tells everyone her age. I find it most unnerving.

**Tom** Unnerving?

**Dodds** Well a woman who will tell you her age will tell you anything. Now, please, Mr Lambert.

**Tom** I do not know Miss Flint's phone number.

**Dodds** Mr Lambert, some of the best liars this country has ever produced have passed through my hands. Politicians, second-hand car dealers, lawyers, insurance agents, tailors, advertising executives, people who write holiday brochures, people who sell hangover cures, police inspectors, lady plumbers ...

**Tom** Lady plumbers?

**Dodds** She was the best liar of the lot. She had a big business in Tring. Took me years to nail her. But look, Mr Lambert ... I'll give you a chance because I'm an old softie when it comes to affairs of the heart. I know why you are reluctant to tell me her phone number.

**Tom** You do?

**Dodds** If she finds out that you are the one who grassed on her, she'll strike you out of her life for ever – so – I'll give you a chance to contact her yourself and tell her to get in touch with me. she knows where I am. (*He shuts his case and gets up*)

**Tom** Look, Mr Dodds ... let's talk about this sensibly. I realize you have your duty to do, and that Joanna has been a big naughty——

**Dodds** Oh she has.

**Tom** I agree, and as a self-employed person she should have paid you tax on what I paid her ... but the tax she owes you, wouldn't buy a small part for Concorde.

**Dodds** I don't get your drift, Mr Lambert.

**Tom** Well ... it seems to me you're chasing peanuts. Does she really merit investigation by a senior inspector such as yourself?

**Dodds** No, on what you paid her it would not justify my superiors assigning me to the case.

**Tom** Then why are you here?

**Dodds** (*collecting up his notes and putting them in his briefcase*) I'm beginning to wonder, Mr Lambert, how well you know her. Surely you knew that Miss Flint has worked for many other people in recent years?

**Tom** For others?

**Dodds** Many others, beside yourself.

**Tom** I ... I ... er ... how do you mean?

**Dodds** I mean that in the last five years your Miss Flint has earned nearly half a million pounds and not paid one penny in tax. Hardly peanuts.

*Tom stares at him. His jaw sags*

Miss Joanna Flint is at the very top of our wanted list. From our point of view she's the most wanted woman in England. I'm looking for the Queen of Peanuts! (*He goes to the door with his case*) Good-day, sir.

*He exits*

*Tom stares after him, watching as he makes his way along the catwalk and vanishes from sight. Tom sits down slowly. He gazes ahead. A slight pause*

*Sarah comes out of the bedroom looking carefully around. She checks Tom is alone and sits beside him*

*He does not move. She takes his hand*

**Sarah** *That's* what I wanted to tell you.

*The* CURTAIN *falls*

# ACT II

*The same. It is a few minutes later*

*Tom is in the same position staring out. He does not seem to have moved a muscle*

*Sarah enters from the kitchen, followed by Albert carrying a tray with coffee cups*

**Sarah** (*determinedly cheerful*) Coffee.

*Tom gives no indication of having heard. They both gaze at him*

**Albert** He's in shock.

**Sarah** Tom?

**Albert** Definite post-taxation trauma. How about a slug of something in the coffee? The brandy's done for, but there's a rather special malt whisky.

**Sarah** (*sitting*) I don't think so.

**Albert** Merely a suggestion. He hides it from me . . . but if you feel the need, it's in the bookcase behind Webster's Dictionary. Shall I be Mother? (*He starts to dispense cream and sugar and hands around the cups during the following*)

**Tom** Sarah?

**Sarah** Yes?

**Tom** In words of one syllable, Sarah, how did Joanna Flint earn all that money?

**Sarah** You can't explain a thing like that in words of one syllable, darling.

**Tom** Try. Do your best.

**Sarah** (*after a pause*) Perhaps I'd better start at the beginning.

**Tom** Yes, please. Slowly.

**Sarah** Well, it began one morning at breakfast. I was having kippers. It was the end of the financial year . . . and there on the table, giving me the evil eye——

**Albert** The kipper?

**Sarah** No. My tax demand. I'd had my first really successful year as an accountant. I thought I'd done very well, until I opened this letter. I owed two years' back tax, and they demanded five thousand on account. I realized that if I continued to be successful I could soon be broke.

*She gets up and walks about. They watch her as she continues*

I thought about it very carefully, and I came to the conclusion that what I needed was some fictitious person, to whom I could pay small sums. Half an hour later I was in Barclays Bank saying to the manager ... "Good-morning. I'm Joanna Flint, and here's a hundred pounds in cash to open my account." He didn't bat an eyelid.

**Tom** He must have said something?

**Sarah** (*moving behind the sofa*) Yes, he said ... "Do you take sugar in your tea, Miss Flint?' From then on she sent me occasional bills. I paid the money into her account, then later on popped down and drew it out again. After a while I got her a Barclaycard, and an account at Harrods.

**Albert** Good move that. Gave her credibility.

**Sarah** I thought so.

**Tom** But you said you invented her for me?

**Sarah** I lied.

**Tom** You invented her for *you.*

**Sarah** Originally. Later I allowed you to use her ... and she sort of ... expanded.

**Tom** Without my knowledge?

**Sarah** You never looked at your return. I said "Sign here" and you just signed. Now your trouble's started.

**Tom** My trouble?

**Sarah** Well, our trouble. (*She sits on the arm of the sofa*) It was a client's Christmas party. You were invited, but you were away on that American lecture tour. I remember having lots of drinks, and feeling a great affection for Joanna ... after all, she was paying for the party. I told one of my clients this ... and the next thing they all seemed to know ... and it was a great joke, non-existent Joanna giving us all a party. Then a month later one of them sent in his tax return, and there it was.

**Tom** What?

**Sarah** Three thousand pounds cash payment to Joanna Flint — consultancy fee for his hotel business.

**Tom** Good God!

**Sarah** I protested. He just laughed, and said why should you and I have the sole use of her.

**Tom** Disgusting.

**Sarah** And then they were all at it. Every one of them put Joanna in their expenses. She was doing public relations, market research, working for authors and builders and deep-sea divers. She was everywhere.

**Tom** Bloody swines.

**Sarah** Next year it was worse.

**Tom** How?

**Sarah** They gave her a rise.

**Tom** Why didn't you tell me this was going on?

**Sarah** I kept hoping they — or she would go away. But she didn't, and soon she was in the super-tax bracket ... except she didn't pay it, of course.

**Tom** I'm shocked, Sarah. I really am shocked. I mean, you're a professional person. You're entitled to sign the back of people's passport photos. How could you have done it? You always had such integrity.

**Sarah** Don't go on at me, Tom.

**Tom** (*going on*) You were so honest. You always told the truth. That was the
problem with our marriage . . . when you told me what you thought of me,
I knew it was the truth. Now you've become a liar and a crook. You've
committed a serious crime. You're a villain.
**Sarah** (*a bit tearful*) I know . . . the whole thing's got out of control . . . she's a
monster . . . I can't cope with her any more.
**Tom** You know what you have to do, Sarah? There is no other way. You'll
just have to go to the tax office and tell Mr Dodds everything. You have no
choice.
**Sarah** Yes. I have thought that.
**Albert** You'll never be able to look at yourself in the mirror again, unless you
go there and make a clean breast of it.
**Sarah** I suppose you're right.
**Albert** And when you've done that, it'll take him a few days to get a
warrant — which will give you time to nip off to Spain.
**Sarah** (*brightening*) Ooooh! That's clever!
**Albert** Yes . . . clear your conscience then clear the country.
**Sarah** That's the answer. That's what I'll do. I'll go and get it over with now.

*Tom looks apprehensive again. Sarah rises and collects her briefcase and
handbag. She gives Tom a kiss*

Don't look so worried, Tom. I'll take all the blame . . . complete honesty.
And it'll totally baffle the tax office because they're not used to it.
**Tom** It's the best policy. Honesty always is.
**Sarah** You're right, darling . . . wish me luck.
**Tom** Good luck. We'll be thinking of you.

*She exits*

*Tom looks after her*

What a great girl!
**Albert** 'Ere, hang on. Something's just occurred to me.
**Tom** What's that?
**Albert** If she tells Dodds everything, it'll drop you right in it.
**Tom** How?
**Albert** You signed those fraudulent tax returns. Who is going to believe you
didn't know what you were signing?

*Tom runs out of the door and along the catwalk. He goes out of sight, then
reappears a moment later dragging Sarah by the arm. They enter*

**Tom** That's right. You can't confess! It'll drop me right in it!
**Sarah** But you said——
**Tom** Never mind what I said. You're just being honest at my expense. You
tell all, bunk off to Spain, and I'm left holding all these dodgy tax returns.
You want to think these things out, Sarah . . . have some consideration for
others.

*She bursts into tears*

**Sarah** I don't know what to do ... I can't stand it ... I've got a terrible headache ... I never want to see you or Joanna Flint again!

*She runs into the bedroom*

*The door slams as Tom makes a move to go after her. He comes back and paces for a moment, frowning and ignoring Albert. He suddenly stops*

**Tom** I've got the answer. The complete answer.

**Albert** You have?

**Tom** We'll kill her.

**Albert** I think that's a bit strong. I know she's a bent accountant, but she is still your wife. Fair do's.

**Tom** Joanna, you fool! Not Sarah.

**Albert** Oh, I am sorry. Kill her, eh? How?

**Tom** A road accident. She can be found in a burnt-out car at the bottom of a cliff.

**Albert** I hate to raise this ... but how do you kill someone who doesn't exist?

**Tom** No wonder you're the world's most unsuccessful actor. No imagination. No initiative. We could bury her at sea.

**Albert** Bury who? Who's going in the canvas bag with the lead weights? I know I haven't played a part for a while, but I'm not that desperate ... specially a non-speaking role.

*Tom paces up and down. Albert watches, restraining himself from speaking*

**Tom** All right, suppose ... (*He stops*) ... suppose Dodds read an announcement in the death column of *The Times*? (*He stares up, visualizing it*) "Flint – on the twenty-third of September. Joanna Flint, former press consultant to well-known botanist Tom Lambert, Ph.D. ... B.Sc. Died peacefully in the Himalayas after short illness."

**Albert** What illness?

**Tom** The rope broke. If you can't say anything constructive, shut up.

**Albert** (*after an injured pause*) I think killing her is asking for trouble. It might lead to all sorts of complications. At the moment the most you can get is a few years for fraud. Or perhaps they'll just give you probation and take everything you own.

**Tom** You're not making me feel any better.

**Albert** My point is, at the moment you can only be nicked for fiddling. Why risk a murder rap? No, no ... what you want here is some lateral thinking. Approach this problem from a totally new direction ...

**Tom** Yes?

**Albert** Don't kill her off. Keep her alive, but place her out of reach where Dodds can't get at her.

**Tom** Where could a woman go where Dodds couldn't find her?

**Albert** Well, if it was a Tuesday ... Russell square Turkish baths.

**Tom** Why Tuesday?

**Albert** That's ladies only day.

**Tom** Albert, I do not want any more frivolous remarks. I am in serious trouble. I'm desperate.

*There is a slight ping from the telephone that makes Tom turn and look at it*

**Albert** I'm sorry, Tom. But I'm not like you. I'm not well enough educated to have a criminal mind.

**Tom** Shh! Did you hear that? (*He moves to pick up the phone. He listens*) Do you think this place could be wired? Has Dodds left something here? (*He runs around, feeling under tables and sifting through the foliage of his trellis plant*)

*Sarah enters. She looks at him for a moment*

**Sarah** What's he doing?

**Albert** He thinks there's a bug in his geranium.

**Tom** It'd be just like Dodds. One of these tiny electronic transmitters. He could be out there now, sitting in a plain van, listening to everything we've said. I heard a definite ping.

**Sarah** That was me on the bedroom extension. It's all right. I've sorted it all out.

*They both stare at her*

**Tom** How?

**Sarah** It's the only possible solution. We produce a woman we can introduce to Dodds as Joanna Flint. A woman willing to admit receiving every penny she is supposed to have received. Once she has said that face to face with Dodds, she can disappear for ever and let them try and find her.

**Tom** (*patiently*) Sarah, that's a brilliant idea. I thought of it hours ago, but I can't think of anyone who would do it.

**Sarah** I can.

**Tom** You can?

**Sarah** I already have. My friend Prudence.

**Tom** (*astonished*) Prudence?

**Sarah** Yes.

**Tom** Prudence thingamy — from Weybridge?

**Sarah** Yes, I've just outlined the problem to her on the phone. I explained why *I* couldn't do it because I'm known at the tax office . . . and when she heard what a spot we were in she said she'd help.

**Tom** (*surprised*) Prudence did?

**Sarah** She is on her way over.

**Albert** Sarah, you're a marvel.

**Sarah** When she arrives we can brief her on all the details.

**Albert** She sounds like a very good friend.

**Sarah** Oh she is, Albert. We were at school together. She won't let us down.

**Albert** And you think she can carry it off?

**Sarah** I'm sure of it. I promised I'll be with her . . . prompting her. All she has to do is confirm what I say. If Dodds doubts her identity she shows him Joanna's Barclaycard.

**Albert** Very good. And then what?

**Sarah** She walks out of his office and he'll spend the next twenty years looking for her.

**Tom** Wait a minute, Sarah.

**Sarah** It's perfect.

**Tom** No, it isn't. In my efforts to make your Joanna credible ... a real woman ... I told Mr Dodds I'd had an affair with her ...

**Sarah** So?

**Tom** I told him Joanna was attractive, and that I adored her.

**Sarah** Well ...?

**Tom** The last time I saw Prudence she was fifteen stone, and had just won the Ladies Amateur Shot-put for Surrey.

**Sarah** Well, she's been on a very strict diet since then, and taken up hurdling.

**Tom** Apart from that, Prudence does not adore me. The last time we met she said how glad she was you had finally got rid of me.

**Sarah** It's true. Prudence does hate you. She doesn't want to help you at all.

**Tom** There you are then.

**Sarah** But I told her we were *both* in a jam. The same jam. If she wanted to help me she couldn't avoid helping you.

**Tom** What did she say to that?

**Sarah** That it was very regrettable ... but since I was her best friend, there was no alternative.

**Tom** In that case, all our problems are solved. She'll convince Dodds she's Joanna Flint. Dodds doesn't stand a chance against Prudence. If he expresses the slightest doubt about her, she'll give him a fourpenny one.

**Albert** Would it be too premature to open a bottle of something in celebration?

**Tom** Not at all. If Prudence is on our side, the battle is already won. It's like having Al Capone saying he's Joanna Flint ... Sarah, it's a stroke of genius.

*The phone rings. A slight pause as they all look at it*

**Albert** I do hope she hasn't changed her mind.

*Albert looks at them both staring at the phone, neither making a move to answer it. Finally Albert does*

(*On the phone*) Hello? ... Yes? (*He puts his hand over the receiver*) It's Dodds.

*No-one moves*

I said it's Dodds. Are you in, or not?

**Tom** (*suddenly nervous*) I'm not sure. (*To Sarah*) Am I in?

**Sarah** Of course you're in. Don't lose confidence. We've now got a real, living Miss Flint.

**Tom** Yes, you're right.

*Tom takes the phone with a brisk confident manner. Sarah follows him to the phone*

(*On the phone*) Hello, Mr Dodds ... nice to hear from you again, so soon. How are you keeping? ... Good. The sun hasn't held its early promise, has it? ... I was just saying to my accountant — ... Yes, that's right. ... Yes, she is here. . . . (*Suddenly nervous again*) Could we what? . . . Pop round to your office. . . . (*He looks enquiringly towards Sarah*)

**Sarah** (*anxiously, prompting*) It's rather short notice.

**Tom** (*repeating into the phone*) It's rather short notice, Mr Dodds. . . . Yes, but I don't know the address.

**Sarah** Two hundred and twenty High Holborn.

**Tom** Two hundred and twenty High Holborn. (*He writes it down*) M Division? . . . We go round the left-hand side of the building. . . . Yes . . .

**Sarah** No . . . no . . . the Investigation Department is on the third floor.

**Tom** Just a moment, Mr Dodds, I've got my accountant with me and she's been there before. . . . yes. . . . Do have a word with her.

*Tom offers her the phone. She takes it reluctantly*

**Sarah** Hello, Mr Dodds? Miss Davenport speaking. . . . Well, yes – if I came with Mr Lambert I might be able to iron out a few wrinkles for you. . . . Oh I see. It's the *Special* Investigation Department, M Division. . . . We go round the back of Head Office and down some steps. . . . Yes. . . . Yes. . . . Yes. . . . We'll be there at three-thirty. . . . (*Stunned*) I beg your pardon? Could you say that again? . . . Yes, we'll be there. Goodbye, Mr Dodds. (*She hangs up and stares at them blankly*) He said his enquiries have taken a new turn.

**Tom** What new turn?

**Sarah** He said he's just been in touch with Miss Flint.

*A long pause*

**Tom** In touch with her?

**Sarah** Yes.

**Tom** But she doesn't exist.

**Sarah** She exists for Dodds. He's just spoken to her.

**Albert** Excuse me, but I'm not quite . . . Is this a turn for the better?

**Tom** He can't have spoken to her. He can't be telling the truth.

**Albert** I thought you said you'd invented her?

**Sarah** I did invent her. She's just a figment.

**Tom** So it must be a bluff.

**Sarah** Or a double bluff.

**Albert** Or a turn for the worse.

**Sarah** What's his game?

**Tom** I don't know, but we mustn't lose our heads.

*Tom and Sarah stare at each other, both deeply worried. They sit down*

**Albert** (*coughing*) Excuse me . . . but tell me if I've got this quite right. Mr Dodds has said that he's been in touch with a figment of Sarah's imagination . . .?

**Tom** }
**Sarah** } (*together*) Shut up.

*Albert subsides in a chair between them. He looks from one to the other*

**Tom** (*finally*) He's trying to trap us.

**Sarah** That's obvious.

**Tom** Look at it from his point of view. He knows that if Miss Flint doesn't exist, we will know he is lying ...

**Sarah** But we will not be sure if he's lying if she does exist.

**Tom** But ... if we pretend to believe him, will that show we are lying to him or will it show he is lying to us?

**Sarah** What we mustn't forget is that if she doesn't exist, he will know that we know he is lying, but as we have said she does exist ...

**Tom** If it's the truth we will say he's lying.

*Albert is gazing from one to the other like a spectator at a tennis match, thoroughly bewildered*

**Albert** Have either of you got an aspirin?

*They ignore him*

**Sarah** I suppose he *is* lying? Just suppose some strange woman has turned up, and said she is Joanna Flint, how would you be able to deny it?

*Tom stares at her. They are both starting to get nervous*

**Tom** Tell you what ... you go to his office, and I'll wait here to explain things to Prudence.

**Sarah** We *both* have to go to his office now we've agreed. It would only make him more suspicious.

**Tom** But——

**Sarah** (*firmly*) No, Albert stays here and waits for Prudence. Because no matter how many Miss Flints Mr Dodds tries to produce, we know we've got the only genuine one. Is that clear, Albert? (*She collects her briefcase and handbag*)

**Albert** (*bemused*) I think so.

**Sarah** So when she arrives, make her feel at home. Give her a cup of tea. Come on, Tom we'll get a taxi on the corner.

*She exits*

**Tom** Use your charm. Explain what's happened. Tell her she's the only light we've got at the end of a very dark tunnel.

*He follows Sarah out*

*Albert remains sitting and gazing blankly in front of him*

**Albert** (*carefully*) If they pretend to believe him ... will it show that they're lying to him ... or will it show they know he is lying to them? (*He gets up and takes out a large dictionary from the bookcase. He reaches in and produces a bottle from behind it. He opens the bottle, gets a glass and pours himself a drink. He then goes to the laboratory table and picks up the pressurized spray used earlier. He inserts the nozzle in the bottle and squirts a shot of water into it. He re-corks the bottle and replaces it in the bookcase, then puts back the dictionary*)

*During this a woman — C. P. Lens — comes into view on the catwalk. She is*

*smartly dressed and carries a handbag. She stops and looks in and watches
Albert*

*He raises the glass and as he is about to enjoy it he sees the woman looking at
him through the picture windows. His hand bearing the glass continues up past
his lips so that he is now holding it up above his head. He looks up at the glass as
if scrutinizing it against the light. Then, apparently satisfied, he sprinkles it into
the nearest pot plant. The woman taps on the glass. Albert answers the door and
lets her in*

**Lens** I'm sorry to disturb you ...
**Albert** Not at all. I've just been giving the plants their daily nutriment.
**Lens** I'm not sure if I have the right address. I'm looking for Miss
Davenport.
**Albert** Yes, I know, I've been expecting you. Sit down. You've just missed
her. I'm a friend of theirs. You didn't waste much time. You're obviously
looking forward to meeting this tax man?
**Lens** Oh, I am.
**Albert** He's been driving us all mad ... his name is Dodds, but I expect Sarah
told you. Listen, I'll just nip out the back, and see if I can catch 'em. Then
you can all go together. Shan't be a tick.

*He hurries off into the kitchen before she can reply. We hear the back door
open and shut*

*Mrs Lens looks after him, puzzled, then goes to the phone and dials a number*

**Lens** (*on the phone*) One seven six please. ... Mr Barnet please. ... This is
Chief Inspector Lens, M Division. ... Hello, Mr Barnet. C. P. Lens here.
Can you tell me which area office Mr Dodds is attached to? There seems to
be a slight lack of liaison somewhere ... It might be one of those chaps
seconded from Newcastle. You know what they're like up there. ... Yes,
I'll hold on ...

*The outside kitchen door is heard opening and shutting. Albert comes in
breathlessly*

**Albert** (*puffed*) Missed 'em.
**Lens** (*calmly, on the phone*) Oh, thank you, I'll speak to him later. (*She hangs
up. To Albert*) I hope you didn't mind me using the telephone?
**Albert** Not at all Prudence. Help yourself. Fancy a cup of tea?
**Lens** No, thank you ...
**Albert** Right. Sit down and I'll get straight on with it. How much did Sarah
tell you? Did she explain this tax dodge in detail ... or did she just tell you
about Joanna and the bank account?
**Lens** Er ... Joanna?
**Albert** Yes. Joanna Flint.
**Lens** Ah yes! I know about her! (*She sits*) But I would like a few more details.
**Albert** Well, tell me what you don't know and I'll fill you in.
**Lens** Better still ... why don't you start at the beginning?
**Albert** Good idea! Then you won't make any mistakes when Dodds
interrogates you.

*As Albert sits down opposite her, she removes a handkerchief from her pocket and puts it in her handbag. She places the handbag on the coffee table between them*

Right here it is, Prudence. You don't mind if I call you Prudence?

**Lens** Not at all.

**Albert** Well Prudence, the thing is that Sarah has been running this very cosy little tax fiddle ... Tom has saved himself a fortune but the whole thing has got a bit out of hand ... Am I going too fast for you?

**Lens** No.

**Albert** Do you want to take notes?

**Lens** No, I've got a very good memory.

**Albert** Well, Sarah invented this woman Joanna Flint, saying she was a public relations consultant. Sarah then went to Barclays Bank as Joanna and opened up a current account ... with me so far?

**Lens** Yes.

**Albert** Well, first Sarah put her on the payroll ...

**Lens** And then Tom put her on the payroll?

**Albert** Exactly.

**Lens** And then a number of other clients put her on their payrolls?

**Albert** Right. You're catching on quick. You're going to be a big success.

**Lens** I am?

**Albert** Yes. Take my word for it. I can see it now. When you and Sarah go to Dodds and she introduces you as Miss Flint ... all their problems will be over.

**Lens** Oh, so that's it? I'm to be this fictitious lady? And I go to see Mr Dodds, the tax man, and admit I've been paid all this money, give him my fictitious address, promise to turn up and then never be seen again?

**Albert** Excellent! Spot on! Tom said you'd be good and I agree with him! You're going to wipe the floor with Dodds!

**Lens** I'll do my best.

**Albert** As long as you remember that *you* are the only genuine Miss Flint, there'll be nothing to worry about.

**Lens** You mean there's another one?

**Albert** No, that's just Dodds trying to undermine them.

**Lens** Oh, I see.

**Albert** You're in the picture now?

**Lens** Yes. Totally in the picture.

**Albert** Good. I don't think I've left anything out. Any questions?

**Lens** No. You've been most helpful, Mr ... er ... I didn't quite catch your name?

**Albert** Well, I'm Albert Whatmore when I come here ...

**Lens** When you come here?

**Albert** Well, I'm several people, of course. Like everybody else these days.

**Lens** Really?

**Albert** Well, aren't you? Don't tell me you haven't got a few aliases tucked up your jumper? You're mad if you haven't.

**Lens** No, I'm just the same person to everyone. What are the advantages of saying you are different people? I'd love to know.

**Albert**  Right! It'll be a pleasure to acquaint you with the facts of multi life. If
you say you are three people you get three times the dole money—not at
the same labour exchange, of course. When you're ill not only do you get
three times the sick benefit, but you can claim for the other two people as
dependent relatives! Having three names also means you get three times
the social life.

**Lens**  How fascinating! And you are three different people?

**Albert**  I was . . . yes.

**Lens**  But not any more?

**Albert**  No. I'm four people now.

**Lens**  Four?

**Albert**  Apart from being Albert Whatmore when I do my little cleaning jobs,
I'm Albert Turner to my wife in Catford . . . Bert Dean to my common-law
wife in Acton . . . Al Crosby to the Catford labour exchange . . . And Fred
Fullerton to my girl friend in Wembley. In fact . . . (*He laughs*) . . . some
days when I wake up, I not only don't remember *where* I am, I don't know
*who* I am.

**Lens**  But you must have some official name?

**Albert**  Oh I've got a professional name. I'm Albert Larkin when I do my act
at the *Queen Adelaide* on Fridays and Saturdays.

**Lens**  The *Queen Adelaide*?

**Albert**  The pub at the end of this road. They don't pay a fortune, but it helps
me keep in practice. I get fifty quid in the hand no questions asked . . . and
all the Guinness I can manage. But what that landlord gets up to is
nobody's business. There's only him and his missis behind the bar, but he
claims wages for five barmaids! He gets all his spirits from his mate who
nicks it from the warehouse, he claims for a mother-in-law whose been
dead ten years. Why the income tax people haven't rumbled him I just
don't know. Well I do know, of course, it's because they're all a load of
wallies! All that lot up at the Inland Revenue. I mean who'd work for the
Inland Revenue if they had any brains? They'd be out in civvy street doing
the tax fiddles like Sarah.

**Lens**  What name do you pay tax under?

**Albert**  (*laughing*) Pay tax? Me! That'll be the day. For the past twenty years
I've told 'em I'm an actor, but I've never earned enough to pay tax. No,
most of my income comes from these little house-cleaning jobs I do. Plus
my evenings at the *Queen Adelaide*. But that's enough about me. Is there
anything else you need to know about Miss Flint?

**Lens**  Not a thing.

**Albert**  Well, that's a good deed for the day. I think I deserve a drink.

**Lens**  Yes, I think you do.

**Albert**  Make yourself at home. They won't be long. (*He goes to the desk
drawer and takes out several notes, which he pockets*) Now that I've got
everything under control . . . I think I'll have a flutter on the four o'clock at
Kempton. I feel a lot luckier than I did an hour ago.

*He gives her a wave and goes off*

*Mrs Lens watches until he has gone then opens her handbag and takes out a tiny tape-recorder like the one used by Dodds. She presses a button to run it back. She stops it then presses the play button. We hear Albert's recorded voice*

**Albert's Voice** Pay tax? Me! That'll be the day.

*She clicks it off and puts the recorder back in her bag. She looks around the room speculatively . . . as if assessing the value of everything. She sees the gap on the wall where the Picasso hung. Now she checks around, notices the plastic bag and opens it. She takes out the Picasso and studies it. The phone rings. She puts the Picasso back in the bag and replaces it where she found it. She hesitates, then decides to answer the phone*

**Lens** Hello. . . . No, I'm afraid she's not here. . . . He's not here either. Can I take a message? . . . You're at the Elephant and Castle with a flat tyre? And you are? . . . Prudence Copley. Are you the Prudence they were expecting? . . . I see . . . the one who was going to masquerade as a tax dodger? . . . You were going to take part in this criminal deception were you, Miss Copley? . . . No, I'm not a friend. I'm C. P. Lens, Chief Investigating Officer, Inland Revenue M Division. And I'd advise you to go straight home and — . . . Hello? . . . Hello?

*She hangs up with a quiet smile of satisfaction. Now she collects her handbag and exits*

*The Lights fade to a Black-out*

SCENE 2

*The same. It is about an hour and a half later*

*Tom is sitting thoughtfully*

*Sarah comes in from the kitchen*

**Tom** What's his game? Why did he get us over there if he wouldn't see us?

**Sarah** There's no trace of Albert, and Prudence should have been here ages ago.

**Tom** (*not listening*) What is he up to? He phones me and says he wants to see us urgently.

*Sarah goes to the phone and dials during this*

We knock on his door and he comes out and says he's in conference and he'll be in touch. I don't like it.

**Sarah** Nor do I.

**Tom** He's definitely up to something.

*Sarah has been listening as the phone rings. Now she hangs up*

**Sarah** Prudence must have been held up in the traffic.

*Tom gets up*

**Tom** Don't keep on about Prudence . . . I think I'm on to it. (*He moves* *restlessly about the room)* Dodds says he's been in touch with Miss Flint. Now ... I've been racking my brains to find the motive for that extraordinary remark. There is only one explanation that fits. He's gone off his head!

*Dodds appears on the catwalk and looks in the glass window, between the pot plants*

*Tom is too engrossed to notice. Sarah sees him*

**Sarah** Tom ... don't look now, but Mr Dodds is right behind you.
**Tom** *(engrossed, not listening)* It's the only explanation that makes sense. Dodds is off his rocker. It's all got too much for him.
**Sarah** *(quietly)* Turn around nice and slowly, and try to act naturally.
**Tom** *(still engrossed)* Sarah, do stop interrupting. I'm trying to give you a rational——*(He jumps as he sees Dodds staring at him from outside)* Aaaaahhhh! *(He turns back and speaks out of the corner of his mouth)* It's Dodds!
**Sarah** I know!

*Dodds gives them a little wave through the glass. They both wave back*

**Tom** *(softly)* What do we do?
**Sarah** Act naturally.
**Tom** Yes, but will he act naturally?
**Sarah** Let him in!

*Tom goes to open the door. Dodds enters with his briefcase*

**Dodds** I am sorry, Mr Lambert. *(To Sarah)* Ahh, Miss Davenport again ...
**Sarah** *(nodding and smiling)* Mr Dodds ...
**Dodds** I do apologize for your wasted journey, but I had an urgent conference.
**Tom** *(solicitous)* We understand. Sit down, Mr Dodds. Take the weight off your feet.
**Dodds** It's not my feet that have been suffering. Oh, what a day.
**Tom** Exhausting?
**Dodds** Dreadful.
**Tom** The day?
**Dodds** No, the inconvenience.
**Tom** Yes, we're sorry about all that.
**Dodds** No, no, Mr Lambert. It's I who am trying to apologize to you.
**Tom** I see.
**Dodds** Inviting you to the office, and then being unable to see you like that. Most discourteous. Particularly in view of what's happened.
**Sarah** What has happened, Mr Dodds?
**Dodds** Didn't she phone and explain?
**Sarah** Who?
**Dodds** Miss Flint.
**Tom** Er ... not yet.
**Dodds** Well then, she may have tried while you were out.

**Tom** (*humouring him*) Of course.

**Sarah** What exactly was she going to explain, Mr Dodds?

**Dodds** That I'd made an appointment with her. She said it would be better if *she* phoned rather than me, because she could clarify the situation.

**Sarah** (*baffled*) I see. (*She sits down*)

**Dodds** Anyway, that's why I'm here. For the appointment. At five o'clock.

**Sarah** She's coming here at five o'clock?

**Dodds** Yes. She said that would be most convenient for all parties.

**Tom** I see.

**Dodds** But it's not quite five yet, is it?

**Tom** No, not quite.

**Dodds** (*checking through papers*) Anyway, everything is under control. (*He stops*) Oh no! I haven't come without my C.fifty-eight? Where's Miss Flint's C.fifty-eight? Do excuse me, Mr Lambert? I must have filed it in the Morgan file. I have all the documents in my car. How embarrassing! You must think me so inefficient. Goodness me ... I haven't mislaid a C.fifty-eight for years. I'll just be a moment. (*He goes to the door*)

**Tom** Mr Dodds ...?

**Dodds** (*stopping*) Yes?

**Tom** (*choosing his words*) You er ... have arranged all this with Miss Flint?

**Dodds** Yes.

**Tom** You actually spoke to her?

**Dodds** Of course. (*Sharply*) I've told you that.

**Sarah** What is the position then? Now that you've made contact with Miss Flint?

**Dodds** Well, if she does what she's agreed to do and signs the affidavit, then of course, it goes higher up ... but the chances are — the way things look — Mr Lambert could be in the clear.

**Tom** I see.

**Dodds** Though I must tell you that when I left here earlier, I was not of that opinion.

**Tom** You weren't?

**Dodds** No, Mr Lambert. I definitely was not. In fact, I had grave doubts about the very existence of Joanna Flint.

**Tom** You did?

**Dodds** Yes indeed. It's an old dodge. We've been dealing with non-existent people for years. But as fast as they invent them, we circumvent them. Sometimes ... and you won't believe this ... they even try to kill them off. But even that doesn't beat us. We exhume the bodies. There was a funeral at West Norwood where we recovered a coffin full of unpaid tax demands.

*He chuckles. They don't*

That's why it was so refreshing ... such a welcome change ... when your Miss Flint actually arrived in my office.

*They just stare at him for a moment*

**Sarah** She arrived ...?

**Tom** In your office?

**Dodds** Yes.

**Tom** What did she look like?

**Dodds** Surely you must know what she looks like.

**Tom** These days!

**Sarah** Mr Dodds, you actually met her?

**Dodds** Yes, I just told you. She came to my office earlier this afternoon. That's why I couldn't see you. I was discussing it with our legal department.

**Sarah** And was Miss Flint . . . helpful?

**Dodds** Very. I have to say, although she's been defrauding us, she turned out to be a most charming and co-operative person.

**Tom** What actually happened?

**Dodds** Well, we discussed the matter . . . I drew up the affidavit and she burst into tears.

**Tom** She cried in your office?

**Dodds** Floods of tears. I really became quite embarrassed. I thought my colleagues would wonder what I was doing to her.

**Tom** What were you doing to her?

**Dodds** Merely explaining that we would have to prosecute. It's a shame. I feel she is a nice girl at heart who has got into bad company. Well, I'll just nip back to the car and get the right C.fifty-eight. (*He goes towards the door*)

*At the same time Lucy appears on the catwalk and they meet in the doorway*

Ahhh . . . the elusive Miss Flint. I'll be back in a moment with the statements.

*Dodds goes off*

**Lucy** Hi.

**Tom** (*to Sarah*) Did you hear what he said?

**Sarah** Yes.

**Tom** He called her Miss Flint!

**Sarah** Yes.

**Tom** Well, this proves it, beyond a shadow of a doubt Dodds has definitely gone bananas. He's seeing Flints everywhere. Surely we can harness this to our advantage?

**Lucy** But I am Miss Flint.

**Tom** Perhaps we can talk him into making me an off-shore island——(*He stops . . . realizes . . . turns to Lucy*) You're who?

**Lucy** Miss Flint.

**Tom** (*a beat*) Not *Joanna* Flint?

**Lucy** Yes.

**Tom** No . . . no . . . no. You're . . . er . . . you're . . .

**Sarah** Lucy. Lucy Napier.

**Tom** That's right. So since when have you been Joanna Flint?

**Lucy** Since three o'clock this afternoon . . . when Mr Dodds rang up and said he was the Inland Revenue, and was I Mr Lambert's public relations lady? Naturally, I said yes. "You are Miss Joanna Flint?" he asked. Naturally, I said yes again.

**Tom** Naturally?

**Lucy** Well, I sensed you'd been up to something with Miss Flint ...

**Sarah** And naturally you wanted to know more?

**Lucy** Yes.

**Sarah** I can understand that ... but how did he get your number?

**Lucy** I left it on Tom's desk. He must have seen it. Anyway, I admitted everything. He kept making these accusations, and I kept admitting to them. I really got him going. I could tell by the rising note of triumph in his voice. So now I know all there is to know. You won't find a better Miss Flint than me. Actually you won't have a chance. I'm the one and only. I made sure of that.

**Tom** How?

**Sarah** (*knowingly*) By going round to his office, of course.

**Lucy** I thought I'd strike while the iron was hot. He was bowled over. He said, "I thought you would have made a run for it, Miss Flint." "No" I said. "No, Mr Dodds. I'm guilty and I have to face the music."

**Tom** This is absolutely wonderful! You've been very clever!

**Lucy** Yes, I thought so.

**Tom** What a fantastic girl you've turned out to be. Not only attractive and nice, but bright, warm hearted, loyal, generous ...

**Sarah** But we're not quite in the clear *yet* are we, Lucy? (*She sits down*)

**Lucy** Almost. Very nearly.

**Sarah** There's just the little formality of you signing the affidavit?

**Lucy** Yes. That's all I have to do.

**Tom** Wonderful. (*To Sarah*) But won't they arrest her?

**Sarah** Not until they can take out a warrant.

**Lucy** And by that time I'll be in New York, with my little memento of our lovely night together.

**Tom** And what a sensational night it was ... what little memento?

**Lucy** Well, I was hoping you'd like to give me a little keepsake.

**Tom** What little thing did you have in mind?

**Lucy** A little thing that was hanging on the wall ... but I don't see it now. I suppose you had to hide it from ... (*She picks up the bag and looks inside*) ... ah, here it is all wrapped and ready to go. Your little Picasso.

**Tom** (*snatching it from her*) You're not having that! This is my pension, and it's worth a fortune!

**Lucy** Hardly. It's not one of his best ones ... (*She shrugs*) ... still ...

**Tom** No ... fair's fair, Lucy. You've been very clever, and I'm more than willing to show my gratitude. Five hundred quid ...

**Lucy** I just wanted a tiny token of your affection.

**Tom** Seven fifty ... in used notes.

**Lucy** (*sniffing*) How sordid to introduce money into our relationship. I suppose that's my trouble, really. I'm just a silly little romantic ...

**Tom** (*violently*) You're not getting it! (*Clutching the bag*) It's the most precious thing I've ever owned. I'm keeping it for my old age——

**Sarah** Tom ...?

**Tom** ——when I'm crippled with rheumatism and no-one wants me——

**Sarah** Tom you have no choice.

**Tom** — and living in one cold room with a leaking tin roof and an outside
lav——

**Sarah** Lucy now has the power to send us both to prison for a long time.

**Tom** A thousand quid. And that's my last word!

**Sarah** (*rising*) All she has to do is tell Dodds we asked her to masquerade as
Miss Flint, and we're for the high jump.

**Tom** Two thousand quid.

**Sarah** We're so much worse off now than we were this morning before we
had *any* Miss Flint. Don't you see that?

**Tom** Two thousand and my car.

**Sarah** You're not in a position to negotiate.

**Tom** It's got two new tyres.

**Sarah** Tom ... she's met Dodds as Miss Flint. Lucy has brought Miss Flint
to life ...

**Tom** (*to Lucy*) You know what you are, don't you? You're a double-
crossing, blackmailing, fiscal Frankenstein! You're just a cheap little two-
timing——

**Lucy** (*furiously*) Right, that does it! Don't bother to persuade him, Sarah.
I've changed my mind.

*Dodds appears on the catwalk and heads towards the front door*

I'll just tell Dodds it's a pack of lies, and leave you to get on with it.

*Dodds raps on the glass door and gives them a little wave. For a second nobody
moves*

**Tom** (*sadly*) And to think less than twenty-four hours ago you were just a
nice girl who rang my bell. (*He puts the plastic bag down on a chair beside
her*)

**Lucy** Thank you. I'll let him in, shall I?

*Lucy goes upstage and opens the door for Dodds. He has a sheaf of documents*

**Dodds** Getting quite chilly out. Radio predicts a storm later. Shall we all sit
down? (*He sits and shuffles through the documents*) Here's the correct
C.fifty-eight Miss Davenport, if you'd like to check the details.

**Sarah** Oh, I'm sure that won't be necessary.

**Dodds** Well, this won't take long. (*He arranges papers on the table and offers
Lucy a pen*) I'd just like you to sign the copies here ... here and here, Miss
Flint, admitting the various sums you earlier stated you had received.

**Lucy** Yes, Mr Dodds.

*She begins signing the papers which he lays before her one by one*

**Dodds** I shall leave with you, Mr Lambert, that part of this lady's affidavit
which concerns the payments you have made to Miss Flint over the years.

**Tom** Thank you.

**Dodds** And I shall give you, Miss Davenport, those sections which appertain
to payments made to Miss Flint by your various other clients.

**Sarah** Thank you.

*Lucy completes signing. Dodds takes out a large rubber stamp and pad and stamps each document. He rises and hands one document to Tom*

**Tom** Thank you.

*Then Dodds hands another document to Sarah*

**Sarah** Thank you.

**Dodds** Well, that concludes my business. (*To Lucy*) You know where you have to report tomorrow, Miss Flint?

**Lucy** Yes . . . your legal department at noon.

**Dodds** That's right. The Holborn office. (*He gives her a card*) Here's the address.

**Lucy** (*apprehensively*) They won't keep me in will they?

**Dodds** (*smiling*) Good heavens, no . . . we have no power to do things like that . . . (*He packs up his papers*) Cheerio, Miss Davenport . . . Mr Lambert . . . I hope I didn't embarrass you with my questions. Nothing personal . . . all part of the day's work. Good-day to you all.

*He exits with his briefcase and closes the door behind him*

*They watch him walk along the catwalk*

**Sarah** Bravo, Lucy. Well done.

**Lucy** Ta . . . wasn't bad, was it?

**Sarah** Very convincing. Didn't you think so, Tom?

*Tom doesn't answer. He picks up the plastic bag with the painting and brings it out. He looks at it*

Tom . . .

**Lucy** There's no point in trying to go back on our deal, you know.

**Sarah** He knows.

**Tom** (*sadly*) Yes, you convinced him all right . . . and if I don't give you this little memento . . .

**Lucy** I could un-convince him very quickly.

**Tom** I'm just saying goodbye to it. (*He puts it back in the bag and gives it to Lucy*)

**Lucy** Is there a back door?

**Tom** (*pointing*) Through the kitchen.

**Lucy** Just in case Dodds is lurking about. We don't want him asking what's in my little green bag, do we? (*She goes to the kitchen door*) Ta-rah, Sarah.

**Sarah** Ta-ra.

**Lucy** Bye, Tom. Lovely party.

*She exits into the kitchen. We hear a door open and shut off-stage*

**Sarah** (*moving to the sideboard*) I think we need a drink.

*Tom does not respond*

It could be worse.

**Tom** And to think I nearly didn't ask her in.

**Sarah** Well, I'm glad you did. Shall we open a bottle of champagne to celebrate?

**Tom** Celebrate what?

**Sarah** Getting rid of Miss Flint. (*She collects the papers from the pouffe and takes them to the desk*) You're in the clear now with the Inland Revenue . . . I'm in the clear . . . all my other clients are in the clear.

**Tom** Yes. And it's all down to me.

**Sarah** You can rest assured, Tom, I'll speak to them very sternly. It's only because of you and your sacrifice that they're not in prison. I'm sure they'll be very grateful to you. (*She puts the papers in her briefcase*)

**Tom** Do you think they'll make a contribution?

**Sarah** Oh, I don't think they'd go that far. But it is more blessed to give than to receive. That thought will give you great satisfaction in the years to come . . . and that's what I think we should drink to. (*She closes her briefcase*)

**Tom** (*shaking his head*) You've convinced me. I'll get the champagne.

*He goes into the kitchen*

*Mrs Lens appears on the catwalk and comes to the door. She now carries a large briefcase. She rings the bell*

*Sarah answers the door*

**Sarah** Good-evening.

**Lens** May I come in? I'm looking for Miss Davenport and Mr Lambert.

**Sarah** I'm Sarah Davenport.

*As Tom emerges from the kitchen with a bottle of champagne*

And this is Mr Lambert.

**Lens** I hope this is not inconvenient. I called earlier, but you were out. My name is Lens . . . C. P. Lens. My card.

*She hands it to Sarah who reads it and reacts. Tom has taken the wire off the champagne bottle*

**Sarah** (*stunned*) "Mrs Cynthia Lens . . . Chief Inspector of Taxes . . ."!

**Lens** M Division.

**Tom** What?

**Lens** May I sit down? (*She does so without waiting for a reply*)

*Tom clutches the champagne bottle, hardly aware of it*

**Tom** Chief Inspector!

**Lens** That's correct. I'm here about the Miss Flint case.

**Tom** Oh . . . you must be from another department . . . you're overlapping. That matter has been handled by Mr Dodds . . .

**Lens** Oh, I see. Has he completed his enquiries?

**Sarah** (*taking a paper from her case*) Yes, Miss Flint was interviewed here a short time ago, and signed this statement.

*She hands it to Mrs Lens, who puts on her glasses and reads it*

**Lens** Oh yes . . . A C.fifty-eight. Admission of liability. Yes, that seems to be in order. Miss Flint is no longer here, I presume?

**Tom** No. And I do think it's a bit thick. I've had the tax department in and out of my home all day.

**Lens** (*calmly*) Mr Lambert, I notice that a picture has been taken down from the wall. Might I ask where is it now?

**Tom** I ... er ... I ...

**Lens** Surely you can't have mislaid an original Picasso?

**Tom** I find that question grossly offensive, and ... and ... you're trespassing ... invading my privacy ... and I must ask you to leave immediately. Your colleague, Mr Dodds, was far more proper ... he had no interest in my personal possessions ... he was only interested in Miss Flint!

**Lens** Mr Lambert, we all know this statement is nothing but a pack of lies.

*She tears up the copy of the affidavit. They stare, stricken*

This affair of Miss Flint is the most outrageous fraud I've come across in my twenty-three years with the Inland Revenue.

**Sarah** I don't understand? Mr Dodds ...

*Albert comes along the catwalk and lets himself in. He is jovial and relaxed as he enters and takes in Lens ... then sees Tom still holding the bottle of champagne*

**Albert** Ahh, Prudence ... I see the champagne is out, so it all must have gone very well. Allow me. (*He takes the bottle from Tom's frozen hand. Totally oblivious to the atmosphere he starts to open it*) Old Prue did the trick, did she? I gave her the background ... didn't I, Prue?

**Lens** Yes, you did. Most helpful.

*During the next, Albert gets out glasses and a tray from the sideboard and pours the champagne*

**Sarah** Albert ... you told her?

**Albert** Everything. Filled her in ... the whole story ... Miss phoney Flint ... how Sarah opened up a bank account for her ... how Tom had her on the payroll ... (*He puts the tray with the champagne glasses down on a table for them and takes a glass for himself*)

**Sarah** Albert ... this isn't Prudence.

**Albert** Pardon?

**Sarah** Tom, would you like to introduce this lady?

*A pause*

Tom!

**Tom** I ... er ... (*He clears his throat*) ... I'd rather not ... my voice is a little ... no comment. I don't think I ... I wish I was dead.

**Lens** My card.

*She hands him a card. Albert holds it at full arm's length*

**Albert** Where's my glasses ...? (*He feels in his pocket and puts them on ... takes a sip of champagne as he reads the card. He then chokes and splutters*) These aren't my glasses! I've never seen these before in my life. (*Backing to the door*) These must be the barman's glasses from the pub ... (*opening the* *door*) ... that's what happened ... I ordered a double Scotch and he switched glasses. I'll just ... er ... yes.

*He exits very hurriedly along the catwalk*

**Lens** (*smiling*) A pity about his glasses, because I was hoping he'd help me identify this woman. (*She takes a snapshot from her briefcase*) Perhaps you'll be so kind. Is this person Miss Flint?

*She remains seated while they slowly approach either side and look at the photo*

**Sarah** Er ...
**Lens** Do you recognize her?
**Tom** Er ...
**Lens** You seem to be having some difficulty.
**Tom** She's got no clothes on.
**Lens** I know ... but would you mind looking at the face, Mr Lambert.
**Tom** Face? Excuse me, but I don't quite understand why you, a lady tax man, are carrying around a nude photo of my Miss Flint in her briefcase! I mean ... is this customary? Or has the computer got it wrong again?
**Lens** You identify her as Joanna Flint? Good. That's all I wanted to know.

*Dodds approaches along the catwalk, carrying his briefcase*

**Tom** Have you nude photos of other taxpayers? Cyril Smith? Ken Livingstone? A close up of me, perhaps? Is this some new form of persecution? (*He sees Dodds*) Thank God! (*He hurries to the door to let him in*) Mr Dodds, will you come in and sort out what is obviously a monumental cock-up. You told me I was no longer involved in this case.
**Dodds** You aren't, Mr Lambert. I only popped back because I had one final question to ask Miss Flint. Where is she?
**Tom** Never mind about that. Just deal with this woman from the income tax who has a briefcase full of dirty pictures.

*Lens gets up from her chair and Dodds sees her*

**Lens** Hello, Harry. Long time no see.
**Dodds** It's a funny thing, Cynthia, but the moment I came in, and got a whiff of perfume, I sensed an ambush. (*He turns. He smiles and gestures gallantly to Sarah*) And thought ... keep calm, Harry ... nothing to get alarmed about. It is merely that Miss Davenport uses "Mitzoucha" as well as Cynthis.

*During this Mrs Lens approaches him*

Well, how are things going in M Division?

*Mrs Lens slaps his face*

**Lens** You bastard!
**Dodds** Steady on, Cynthia. No need to discuss our little inter-office differences in front of these good people.
**Lens** You pig's bum!
**Dodds** Now come on, remember the motto of the department. "Severity with

Civility." Why not come out and sit in my car? I'm sure we can settle this case quietly ...
**Lens** I knew it was you.
**Dodds** I'm certain we can reach an amicable solution.
**Lens** Mr Dodds, eh? Dodds! Where did you get that name? Last month it was Leadbeater. Before that you were Mr Whitney-Jones ...
**Tom** Excuse me ... what's going on?
**Sarah** Yes, what is going on? Who is he?
**Lens** Well, he's been three different men since last June, and before that, for seventeen years, he was my husband.
**Dodds** Quite.
**Lens** Until he ran off with that temporary little tart we had in the office.
**Dodds** Holiday relief, actually.
**Tom** I'm sorry... I know we've had a long day, but... you did say you were a tax inspector.
**Dodds** I did. Perfectly true. I *was* a tax inspector.
**Lens** Then he left in a huff because they turned him down for the Chief Inspector's job. A month later I got the job, so he left me as well.
**Dodds** Look, Cynthia, we don't have to wash——
**Lens** I just knew it was you ... it had to be ... you swine.
**Dodds** —our dirty linen in public.
**Lens** Where is she? Where is your little floozy?
**Dodds** Well, that's what I came back for actually. But she obviously isn't here, so I'll leave you in peace. (*He goes casually to the door*)
**Lens** You walk out that door, and I'll go straight to the police. I've got enough on you to get you ten years.

*He stops*

Oh yes ... you two have been a great team ... you and that Lucy.
**Tom** A team? You mean they work together?
**Sarah** It was a con-trick?
**Tom** You mean the Lucy who rang me up about market research ... the one I invited in for a drink ... the pair of them were in it together?
**Lens** They've been defrauding smarter people than you up and down the country. It's very easy if you have access to a photocopy machine and my files. When did you actually photostat the files, Harry?
**Dodds** In my lunch hour during my last week, after twenty-nine years' devoted service. I selected three of the special priority red files, put them in a suitcase and took it to be left luggage at Waterloo Station. Naturally, I only bothered to pick those where we were positive of corruption. Like Miss Flint, for instance.
**Lens** (*to Sarah*) Yes, we were building up a nice dossier on her. We expected to nab the lot of you next year... until Harry jumped the gun. Of course, it was no problem for him. He's been knocking on doors, making faces twitch for years.
**Dodds** Now Cynthia ...
**Lens** So it was easy for him. He knew the ropes. I mean, he spent a lifetime

collecting for Her Majesty ... it was quite an easy transition to start collecting for himself.

**Dodds** Now then, old girl ...

**Lens** Don't old girl me, you weasel! (*To Sarah and Tom*) I wasn't here checking on you today ... I was checking on *him*. In fact I've used up my entire annual leave tracking him down. I was too late with that antique dealer last week in Lewisham ... (*to Dodds*) ... you and your floozy got six Chippendale chairs out of him. Don't deny it. And that trick you pulled with the dentist in Mayfair. Taking twenty-seven ounces of gold fillings in lieu of back tax. The Inland Revenue's name absolutely stinks in Mayfair now.

**Dodds** Well, it was never top of the pops before I went there. Be honest.

**Lens** Don't you tell me to be honest! You've sold the entire Inland Revenue down the river. You were everyone's dream! The bribable tax collector! And as for your accomplice – where is that lying little tart?

**Dodds** Well, that's it. That's why I came back. I've got an uneasy feeling that she's been waiting for the right one to give me the elbow. I think she's done a bunk with my Picasso.

**Tom** *Your* Picasso?

**Dodds** (*ignoring him*) I was looking forward to keeping that for my old age.

**Tom** Am I going insane?

**Dodds** (*ignoring this*) We arranged to meet down outside the Co-op. We were going to drive to Paris, and then toddle off down to Monte Carlo and lay low for a bit. But I think that plan might need a little adjusting.

**Lens** Why?

**Dodds** Because as I was waiting I saw a red Porsche stop at the lights. At the wheel was a man who looked like Robert Redford, and beside him, clutching a green parcel, was a young lady who looked awfully like Lucy Napier. I thought I'd better pop back – just to check.

**Lens** So what do you intend to do now? Give yourself up to the police, or make a run for it?

**Dodds** An excellent question.

*Tom dials the phone*

**Lens** What are you doing, Mr Lambert?

**Tom** What any other law-abiding citizen would do. Phoning the police.

**Lens** I see. You wish to go to prison with Harry, do you?

**Tom** I have done nothing in comparison with Harry. All I did was unwittingly claim for Miss Flint ...

**Lens** Up to this morning. Since then you have performed a much more serious crime. You have conspired with others to present a person named Joanna Flint to the Inland Revenue, knowing her to be an imposter. I will deal with you in a moment. In the meantime, sit down and allow me to conduct this enquiry.

**Tom** I——

**Lens** I have to warn you, Mr Lambert, that anything you say in the future will be taken down, and might be used as evidence against you.

*Tom, daunted, sits*

Your future intentions, Harry.

**Dodds** Who else suspects me at the office?

**Lens** No-one. And to avoid any speculation about you, I told them you were now sailing round the world in a friend's boat. You had resigned the service in order to carry out a lifetime's ambition.

**Dodds** Ah!

**Lens** The place is in an uproar, of course. Everyone flying about accusing each other. The current feeling is that it was one of those people made redundant last year. George Truscott is the favourite—especially as he dropped dead last week.

**Dodds** He always was a most obliging fellow. (*A beat*) Would I be correct in assuming that you are the only one who can put the finger on me?

**Lens** Yes. I made a point of handling this matter personally. I asked the Lewisham antique dealer to describe the bogus tax inspector and he said he was a big man with a lot of dark hair.

**Dodds** Ah yes! That was this! (*He produces a black wig from his briefcase*)

**Lens** Then I asked that Harley Street dentist what the tax inspector looked like, and he said he wore glasses and had a large moustache . . .

*Dodds produces them*

Quite.

**Dodds** So nobody else is involved?

**Lens** Just myself, and these good people.

**Dodds** This was going to be my last job, Cynthia. I've used up all my files. Miss Flint was to be my swan song.

**Lens** My duty is clear, Harry. I must inform the fraud squad that I have now identified the bogus tax collector as Harry Lens, my husband.

**Dodds** I agree. That is your clear duty.

**Lens** You will probably get a minimum of five years.

**Dodds** I will.

**Lens** And I will miss you.

**Dodds** I will miss you too, Cynthia.

**Lens** I have missed you very much for the past six months. It is not easy to start a new relationship at my time of life—especially if you are a tax inspector.

**Dodds** I know! I know!

**Lens** I have tried since you left me, but every time I tell a man I am a chief investigating officer for HM Inland Revenue, the relationship does not seem to maintain its early promise.

**Dodds** I'm in the same boat, old girl. I realize now that Lucy was only interested in me for what she could get out of me. All her life she's wanted a red Porsche, you see. The moment she got it, she was off.

**Lens** All the years I've known him he's never fancied young girls before.

**Dodds** I know it's been a madness.

**Lens** It just isn't him.

**Dodds** I've always known that tax inspectors marry tax inspectors.

**Lens** They do. We always marry our own kind.

**Dodds** Like that undertaker who lives opposite us in Tulse Hill.

**Lens** Yes. He married another undertaker's daughter.

**Dodds** He and I always have to drink together at the local, because no-one else will.

**Lens** And when his wife gives dinner parties, we're the only guests! I'm the only housewife in our street who turns up at her Tupperware parties. (*She sniffs and fumbles for her hanky*) We're social pariahs!

**Dodds** We've only got each other, Cynthia.

**Lens** We have! We have!

**Dodds** (*quickly*) So I'll come home then?

**Lens** You mustn't feel you have to.

**Dodds** I need you, Cynthia. Do you need me?

**Lens** The sash-cords have gone again in the kitchen.

**Dodds** I'll fix 'em. There's a new nylon sash-cord someone told me about. I'll try that this time.

**Lens** And what about the money you made?

**Dodds** I only ever swindled the swindlers. Money they owed to the Inland Revenue.

**Lens** Then you must send it to the Inland Revenue.

**Dodds** I will — anonymously in a brown paper parcel.

**Lens** Good. And you will reform, and get a proper job?

**Dodds** I thought I'd become a tax consultant. There's a big future in evasion.

**Lens** You won't do anything to embarrass me?

**Dodds** Never again.

**Lens** Then you'd better come home, Harry.

**Dodds** Yes, Cynthia.

*They kiss, then collect their briefcases and go to the door*

**Tom** Just a moment! You can't just walk out of here like that. We've heard you admit you're a bogus tax officer. The man's an out-and-out criminal. I can't allow that. I'm a respectable citizen. I even had a Picasso. There's a lot of questions to be asked. For instance . . . what's happened to it?

**Dodds** We'd all like to know that one.

**Tom** She's got to be arrested.

**Dodds** How? Where do you suggest we look?

**Tom** Well . . . (*at a loss, then he sees the number on the desk*) . . . for a start, I'll try this phone number.

**Dodds** I would — if you want some fish and chips. They should be open soon.

**Tom** You don't really think you'll get away with this?

**Sarah** We know everything about him. After all, we went to his office at the Inland Revenue.

**Tom** He came out and told us he was too busy to see us.

**Sarah** And then he went back into his office.

**Lens** Harry!

**Dodds** Well. It was the Boiler Room.

**Tom** Boiler Room? I saw the sign on the door. "Gilbert Dodds, Special Investigator, M Division Inland Revenue."

**Dodds** Yes, I stuck it up with Bluetac just before you arrived. It said "Boiler Room" underneath.

**Lens** (*fondly*) Oh Harry ... you are a clever swine.

**Tom** But why get us there in the first place?

**Dodds** Because it terrifies guilty people when they get summoned to Head Office.

**Lens** And rightly so!

**Tom** It's monstrous that he should go scot-free after what he's done, and I should lose my Picasso because of the little fiddle I've done.

**Sarah** It is! Monstrous!

**Lens** I agree.

**Dodds** So do I.

**Lens** I really am very sorry for you, Mr Lambert.

**Tom** (*surprised*) You are?

**Lens** Very. I think you've come out of this very badly.

**Dodds** Most unjust.

**Lens** Mind you, there is a poetic justice about you losing your Picasso.

**Tom** A poetic justice?

**Lens** Did the painting cost you more than fifteen thousand pounds?

**Tom** No.

**Lens** Well, that's what you saved in tax by your fraudulent claims for Miss Flint. You bought it with our money, in fact.

**Dodds** Not only that, you are still in profit.

**Tom** No ... no ... I'm not having that.

**Sarah** Certainly not.

**Tom** Not after your accomplice has made off with my Picasso.

**Sarah** We won't even waste time talking to them, Tom. Phone the police, right now.

**Tom** Right.

**Lens** And tell them what?

**Tom** Everything! How your husband swindled me out of a valuable painting ... how I was forced to give it to this woman because I needed her to pose as my public relations ... (*he stops*) ... well, we needn't dwell on that. I'd say he came into my house posing as a bogus tax man because I'd ... because Sarah had invented this Miss Flint ... (*He stops again, makes a determined effort*) Actually, all that is beside the point. I'll tell them how *he* went up and down the country swindling innocent taxpayers ... and they would only have to phone up the Inland Revenue and talk to the officer in charge of this enquiry ... (*He stops*)

**Lens** Which is me.

**Tom** (*flummoxed*) Yes.

**Lens** And then? Do tell me what you'd do next, Mr Lambert? If there is a loophole I'd like to know it.

**Tom** Sarah ... you're my accountant ... is there a loophole?

**Sarah** No.

**Lens** I'm so glad you agree. I really believe it's stalemate. You can't touch Harry. I can't touch Miss Flint. So much as it hurts me, Miss Flint will have to be disposed of.

**Tom** We've been trying to do that all day.

**Lens** Yes, but you have expert professional help now. After all, we know what we can believe.

**Tom** (*to Sarah*) Do they?

**Sarah** Oh yes.

**Lens** There are certain cases where the tax evader slips the net completely.

**Dodds** Yes there are. Rare circumstances where the Inland Revenue has to concede the game. (*To Lens*) Is this a B.O.F.M. perhaps?

**Lens** I think so. (*To Tom and Sarah*) Miss Flint will soon be writing to us from the little village of Piedra Sola, saying she is unable to return to the United Kingdom to answer our enquiries. She is now married and no longer a British citizen.

**Dodds** She's become the Marquesa Joanna Maria Gianola—formerly Flint. That should close the file.

**Lens** Yes, we always close the file when we get a B.O.F.M.

**Tom** What's a B.O.F.M.?

**Lens** A Bugger Off From Montevideo. (*She goes to the door*) Now come along, Harry. I've got a lot more to say to you . . .

**Dodds** (*accompanying her*) Yes, dear.

**Lens** Those gold fillings have got to go straight back where they came from.

**Dodds** (*as he exits*) Yes, dear. I'll send everything back . . . including the six Chippendale chairs.

**Lens** (*as she exits*) I've been wondering about those. They would look very nice in our dining-room . . .

*They exit*

*Tom and Sarah watch them until they vanish from sight*

**Tom** (*after a pause*) Sarah?

**Sarah** Yes, Tom?

**Tom** I think the entire world is bent! I didn't yesterday. I do today. When I next get the bill for my rates, I'll give the town clerk a tenner, and he'll say this flat doesn't exist. They're all crooks! All imposters! Milkmen, traffic wardens. The next time I get breathalysed . . . when they take me to the station, I'll simply say to the officer in charge . . . "Here's a fiver, Sergeant . . . would you pee in the bottle for me?" (*He flops down in a chair. Sighs*) My poor Picasso. (*The emotion makes him blow his nose vigorously*) My Poor priceless Picasso. My only nest egg . . . and it's been scrambled.

*Sarah comes and sits on the arm of the chair beside him*

**Sarah** I wonder what that Picasso is really worth?

**Tom** It goes up every year. You told me it would when you persuaded me to buy it. When you introduced me to that man who was Picasso's butler. Bargain of a lifetime, you said. That's why I sold all my insurance policies to rake up the seven thousand pounds he wanted.

**Sarah** That's true. But I began to wonder when he went to jail soon afterwards.

**Tom** Went to jail?

**Sarah** Yes. He got six years.
**Tom** (*with growing uneasiness*) What for?

*She doesn't reply*

Murder? Rape? If you tell me it was forgery, I'll kill you.

*She strokes his head, perched beside him*

**Sarah** That's the trouble with you, darling . . . that's why I didn't mention it. You do so hate being told bad news.

CURTAIN

# FURNITURE AND PROPERTY LIST

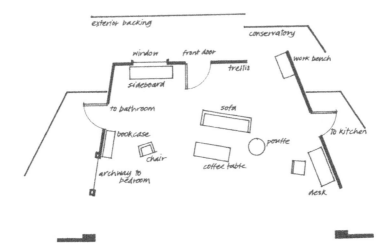

## ACT 1

### Scene 1

*On stage:* Sofa. *Behind it:* pair of tights
Leather armchair
Sideboard. *In it:* bottle of brandy, glasses, tray
On wall above sideboard: Picasso drawing with light above
Desk. *On it:* telephone, magnifying glass, address book, papers, pens
Swivel chair
Pouffe
Coffee table
Bookcase. *On shelves:* silver bowl, books including a large dictionary
Workbench. *On it:* plants, horticultural equipment, specimen jars. *Next to it:* plastic noteboard
In conservatory: long pruning pole
Trellis with climbing plants. *On it:* **Lucy**'s knickers
On walls: photographs, pictures, paintings
Carpet
Window curtains (*half-drawn*)
Scattered around room: empty bottles, glasses, used plates, tray, full ashtrays, **Lucy**'s clothes, satchel bag, fur-coat and files

Waste-paper bin
Cupboard. *In it:* coat-pegs, vacuum cleaner (*practical*), towel

*Off stage:*  Toothbrush **(Lucy)**
Grip **(Albert)**
Handbag, briefcase containing glasses, papers, files incl. one containing a letter **(Sarah)**
Tray with two cups of coffee, cream-jug, sugar-bowl, spoons, Eccles cakes **(Albert)**
Satchel bag **(Lucy)**

*Personal:*  **Albert:** key in pocket


## SCENE 2

*Strike:*  Tray with coffee cups etc., vacuum-cleaner

*Set:*  Plant spray for **Albert**
Empty brandy bottle and 2 empty glasses on coffee table
Green plastic bag on workbench

*Off stage:*  Handbag, briefcase **(Sarah)**
Briefcase containing papers, pen, booklet, mini tape-recorder **(Dodds)**

*Personal:*  **Tom:** address book in pocket, wrist-watch
**Albert:** key in pocket


# ACT II

## SCENE 1

*Set:*  **Sarah's** briefcase and handbag by sofa
Bottle of whisky behind dictionary in bookcase
Money in desk drawer

*Off stage:*  Tray with 3 cups of coffee, cream-jug, sugar-bowl, spoons **(Albert)**

*Personal:*  **Lens:** handbag containing tape-recorder, handkerchief in pocket

## SCENE 2

*Strike:*  Tray with coffee cups etc.
**Albert's** dirty glass

*Set:*  **Sarah's** briefcase by desk

*Off stage:*  Briefcase containing papers, pens, rubber stamp and ink pad, address cards **(Dodds)**
Sheaf of documents **(Dodds)**
Briefcase containing glasses, address cards, snapshot **(Lens)**
Bottle of champagne **(Tom)**
Briefcase containing black wig, glasses, false moustache **(Dodds)**

*Personal:*  **Lens:** handkerchief
**Albert:** key, glasses in pocket
**Tom:** wrist-watch, handkerchief

# LIGHTING PLOT

Property fittings required: picture light
Interior. A studio/apartment. The same scene throughout

ACT I, SCENE 1    Morning

*To open:* Gloomy interior lighting

| | | |
|---|---|---|
| *Cue* 1 | **Tom** draws back curtains<br>*Bring up general interior lighting* | (Page 2) |
| *Cue* 2 | **Tom:** "She hung up."<br>*Fade to Black-out* | (Page 19) |

ACT I, SCENE 2    Early afternoon

*To open:* General interior lighting

*No cues*

ACT II, SCENE 1    Mid-afternoon

*To open:* General interior lighting

| | | |
|---|---|---|
| *Cue* 3 | **Lens** exits<br>*Fade to Black-out* | (Page 43) |

ACT II, SCENE 2    Late afternoon

*To open:* General interior lighting

*No cues*

# EFFECTS PLOT

## ACT I

Cue 1    After CURTAIN rises      (Page 1)
*Music from ice-cream van, off: "Greensleeves" – played very quickly; break off abruptly; pause, then resume music*

Cue 2    **Tom** (*off*): "Shut up!"      (Page 1)
*Stop music; pause 4 seconds, then resume music*

Cue 3    **Tom**: ". . . woken me up."      (Page 1)
*Stop music; pause, then **Man's voice** singing "Just one Cornetto!",*
*then "Greensleeves" music*

Cue 4    **Tom**: ". . . a knuckle sandwich!"      (Page 2)
*Stop music*

Cue 5    **Tom** comes back in      (Page 2)
*Few bars "Colonel Bogey"*

Cue 6    **Tom** runs out      (Page 2)
*Van starts up and drives off*

Cue 7    **Tom**: "I remember it well."      (Page 3)
*Telephone rings*

Cue 8    **Lucy** clutches on to trellis      (Page 4)
*Slight creak*

Cue 9    **Albert** hangs up mac and surveys debris      (Page 4)
*Sharp crack of splintering wood*

Cue 10    **Albert** admires **Lucy**'s rear view      (Page 4)
*Sharp crack of snapping wood*

Cue 11    **Lucy** lowers her leg to a lower rung      (Page 4)
*Another crack*

Cue 12    **Lucy**: "Help! I'm falling."      (Page 4)
*Loud crack*

Cue 13    **Albert**: "Instant coffee."      (Page 10)
*Telephone rings*

Cue 14    **Dodds** switches on tape recorder      (Page 27)
*Tape of **Tom's voice**: "No, I've never even heard of Miss Flint."*

## ACT II

Cue 15    **Tom**: "I'm desperate."      (Page 35)
*Slight ping from telephone*

MADE AND PRINTED IN GREAT BRITAIN BY
LATIMER TREND & COMPANY LTD PLYMOUTH
MADE IN ENGLAND

Lightning Source UK Ltd.
Milton Keynes UK
UKOW06f2109260315

248597UK00001B/5/P